Trends in Linguistics

State-of-the-Art Reports

edited by

W. Winter

University of Kiel, Germany

2

ISBN 90 279 3064 3

Printed in the Netherlands

PREFACE

Many people think of literacy primarily in terms of pre-literate or semi-literate societies. Here, I have taken the term in its basic meaning — the skill of reading and writing in any context. Because it was in the US that linguistics was first applied to problems of literacy, the book begins with materials from the US. The second section focuses on ethnic languages. The final section presents in some detail my own theoretical framework and method which are, as far as I know, the only examples of complete application of linguistics to literacy.

In writing this book I have been overwhelmed by the sheer volume of material that has been written on linguistics and literacy, and on closely related topics. Although I looked at well over 400 items (more than 300 of which are in the bibliography of this volume), I am fully aware that I did not exhaust all of the possibilities. I had deliberately limited myself to the literature of the United States and to work in the ethnic languages (ignoring other developments, as for instance in Australia and Europe), but even within the field thus limited it is no longer probable that one can find exhaustively all the references for an expanding topic like this one. I ask the reader's indulgence, therefore, for the gaps in the coverage. And if, in reducing whole books to a sentence or two of annotation, I have twisted the author's meaning, or missed his major contribution, I can only hope that some reader will publish the articles that will remedy the error.

I acknowledge my debt to Susan Harris who did the essential library search, to Elaine Good whose typing and retyping made completion of the manuscript possible, and to Pamela White who undertook the thankless job of checking and correcting the bibliographical entries. I am also indebted to my colleagues of the Summer Institute of Linguistics, Inc., who have shared in the development of my own materials, and who have provided a sounding board for the final section of this book.

May, 1974   Sarah C. Gudschinsky

INTRODUCTION

The purpose of this small book is to survey the impact of linguistics on literacy, providing enough annotated bibliography so that the interested reader can continue to study the subject in greater depth. In gathering bibliography for this purpose, I found myself hopelessly ethnocentric, writing only about the areas of which I have some first-hand knowledge and easy access to the literature. But even within this limited range, I find my subject, and consequently the book, divided into two distinct parts: (1) Linguistics and literacy in the United States; and (2) Linguistics and literacy in the ethnic languages of the world. Although my own contribution belongs logically with part 2, it is so different from anything else that is being done that I have chosen to give this topic a section of its own: (3) A fully linguistic method. Part 3 differs from the rest of the book in style as well as content. Whereas parts 1 and 2 are essentially a review and annotation of the literature, part 3 is an original exposition of my own work: 3.1 provides a pedagogical outline of the method, and 3.2 describes the necessary linguistic input.

Certain biases that are evident throughout the book should be explained here. These include my view of literacy, the particular linguistic theory within which I work, and the meaning of what I have chosen to call *ethnic languages*.

The exact meaning of the term *literacy* is a source of contention among those who discuss this subject. Is literacy the bare ability to read and write? Or does it include other basic skills such as arithmetic? Or does it imply a certain standard of education such as 4th grade or 6th grade? Is a person literate when he can reproduce the literal meaning of the message on a printed page? Or does literacy imply a certain level of skill in critical judgment or aesthetic enjoyment? I have chosen to resolve this difficulty by the use of my own definition:

That person is literate who, in a language he speaks, can read with understanding anything he would have understood if it had been spoken to him; and can write, so that it can be read, anything that he can say. (Gudschinsky 1968: 146)

This definition reflects my conviction that literacy is a skill, a tool, a means

1

LINGUISTICS AND LITERACY IN THE UNITED STATES

Since the mid-fifties, the theory and practice of literacy teaching in the United States has been in turmoil. On the one hand there is widespread dissatisfaction with old methods and values. On the other hand there is widespread dissatisfaction with the plight of ethnic minorities and the "disadvantaged" children of the inner city. These dissatisfactions have spawned a spate of new materials, new programs, and new theories. Linguists and linguistics have had a role both in fomenting dissatisfaction and in developing new programs and new models of the reading process.

Section 1.1 discusses the methods of teaching literacy, both traditional methods and the newer linguistic methods, and the continuing debate about method. Section 1.2 discusses the contribution of psycholinguistics: the new models of the reading process and the studies in orthography, grammar, language acquisition, and perception that have a bearing on literacy. Section 1.3 discusses the contribution of sociolinguistics, and bilingual and dialect education in the United States.

1.1 METHODS OF TEACHING LITERACY

1.1.1 Traditional methods

The contribution of linguistics to literacy teaching is best understood in terms of a change from traditional methods. This section, therefore, surveys those traditional methods which were already in use before linguistic findings became readily available to the educators — and before "linguistics" had become a popular "in" word. There are a number of excellent summaries of the history of reading methods, so only a brief mention of the highlights is given here. The interested reader should see: Fernald (1943: 21-9); N.B. Smith (1934), and Fries (1962: 1-34). The outstanding characteristic of these histories of method in teaching reading is the *déjà vu* with which the historian sees each new innovation in turn. There does not appear to be anything really

own son was having reading difficulties in the traditional methods being used for teaching reading in the schools at that time. He devised a method for helping him based on one-syllable words and pseudo-words grouped in contrasting sets similar to the "families" of earlier teaching methods. His method for using these materials was to have the child spell the word first and then pronounce it. Basic to this method is the separation of the problem of word-form recognition from the problem of word-meaning. From Bloomfield's point of view, the child entering school already has had five or more years of experience in acquiring word meanings and already has a large inventory of words that he knows — at least five thousand and possibly as many as twenty-five thousand. His problem is not to develop an ability to learn word meanings, but to learn to recognize the word forms when he sees them. The method differs from phonics instruction in that the grouping of the words makes the patterns obvious, so that the child does not need to learn specific rules.

Bloomfield wrote an essay on his method for teaching reading, and collaborated with Clarence Barnhart in preparing materials. However, since the method went so directly against everything that educators and psychologists thought they knew about the teaching of reading, Bloomfield was unable to find a publisher for his essay until 1942, when it was finally accepted by *The elementary English review* (Bloomfield 1942). Even the publication of the article, however, did not pave the way for any widespread recognition of Bloomfield's contribution. He and Barnhart continued to look for a commercial publisher for materials that they had developed but were unable to find one. The materials were used on a very small scale in a few individual classrooms between 1942 and 1961 when they were finally published (Bloomfield - Barnhart 1961).

It should be evident that the method that Bloomfield was suggesting is "linguistic" only in its contrast to the artificiality of the traditional phonics rules on the one hand, and its contrast to the look-say method which largely ignores the alphabetic nature of the English orthography on the other hand. The contribution is based solidly and exclusively on the notion of 'phoneme'. This is perhaps not surprising in the light of the fact that it was the discovery and development of the phoneme which was the great impetus for the development of linguistic science in the thirties.

Bloomfield's point of view had small hearing and no real impact on the teaching of reading during his lifetime.

Other early linguistic work related to literacy (Bolinger 1946, Pulgram 1951, H. L. Smith 1958) was also ignored. In 1946 Bolinger broke with the linguistic shibboleths of his time and wrote an article insisting that visual morphemes exist at their own level, independently of vocal-auditory morphemes. He develops four lines of evidence that the fluent reader indeed reads visual morphemes which are not directly related to his vocal-auditory morphemes. This might have had some bearing on the long standing argument as to whether reading should be primarily a process of equating letters with sound or primarily a process of getting meaning directly from the printed page. There is no evidence, however, that this particular article had any major influence on the educators.

Pulgram (1951) prefigured discussions in which graph-grapheme are compared with phone-phoneme. His material was ignored by educators, but it might not have been very useful to them since he did not see the relationship of two spellings of the same sound to each other – but only the relationship of different forms of the same letter to each other. (For a quite different treatment of some of these problems see section 3.2 "Linguistic base".)

H.L. Smith's *Linguistic science and the teaching of English* (H.L. Smith 1956) includes a rather full discussion of the distress of linguists who saw the reading methodology of that time as completely unrelated to spoken language, or the processes by which language is acquired by the speaker. He grants that reading is more than a decoding skill and that the word and ₎sentence methods have in their favor the fact that the speaker learns sets and patterns before he learns isolates. On the other hand he points out that a lack of knowledge of the relationship between the written language and the spoken language makes the teacher's work very much more difficult. He also notes that although the larger patterns may be learned first, the isolates must eventually also be learned. He also points out that the writing system of English is incomplete and inconsistent – and that it is the task of the linguist to provide for the educator a detailed study of these cases of inconsistency and incompleteness.

By the mid-fifties there was a widespread dissatisfaction with the teaching of reading in the American schools, so that the stage was set for a fresh swing of the pendulum. Into this climate of opinion came the popular book by Rudolph Flesch *Why Johnny can't read* (Flesch 1955). The book is an emotional and persuasive criticism of the look-say method of teaching reading and a ringing call to return to phonics and primary emphasis on the decoding skills – "simply sounding out". Flesch's thesis is that since English is written with an alphabetic orthography, learning to associate the letters of the orthography with the sounds of the language will automatically result in adequate reading.

The book aroused in American laymen a great surge of interest in what was going on in the schools and opened a heated debate in the ranks of the educators. It was this hot debate which provided the climate in which at last a linguistic contribution could be heard. For the first time the big publishers, the educators, and the public at large were ready to listen to new ideas. Oddly enough, Flesch in his desire to reinstate phonics as a primary teaching method credits his reading of Bloomfield's article with stimulating his original interest. Bloomfield, of course, was as deeply opposed to phonics as he was to word or story methods.

By 1958, Barnhart was able to get a grant which enabled him to revise and develop the Bloomfield teaching materials and get them published, and three years later *Let's read* appeared (Bloomfield - Barnhart 1961). It included an updated version of Bloomfield's materials, a printing for the first time of the whole of Bloomfield's own essay on linguistics and reading (Chapter 4 "Teaching children to read"), a detailed history of the Bloomfield system, and an introduction for teachers by Robert C. Pooley. The commercial materials were published in a trial edition (Bloomfield - Barnhart 1963); in this form the materials have received wide-spread attention and some testing in various school systems.

The Bloomfield - Barnhart contribution to the teaching of reading might be summarized in the following points:

(1) The first task in learning to read is learning the alphabetic principle. Meaning will come naturally as soon as the code is understood.
(2) The mastering of the code can be facilitated by using the regular relationships between sound and spelling, avoiding the high frequency irregular words like *look, come, go, to,* etc. Oral reading should be stressed, and the use of pictures avoided.
(3) Words should be read as wholes. In this he agreed with the look-say methods and disagreed with the phonics methods. However, his insistence on the spelling of the words is diametrically opposed to the look-say notion of recognizing the word as a whole apart from its letters.

Soffietti develops and defends Bloomfield's point of view on the teaching of reading. His primary emphasis is that

[...] while the reading specialist is inclined to say, 'The printed word merely acts as the trigger that releases a meaning we already possess,' [...] the linguist believes that the printed word acts as the *trigger that releases its oral counterpart*, which, in its turn, releases a meaning we already possess. (Soffietti 1955: 69)

Charles Fries was an eminent linguist whose primary work was in the historical and descriptive study of the English language. He had, however, long been occupied with applied linguistics as well, especially in the application of linguistics to the teaching of English as a foreign language. In the early sixties he turned his considerable scholarly talent to the application of linguistics to problems of teaching reading. His *Linguistics and reading* (Fries 1962) is an attempt to bring the developing science of linguistics to bear on problems of teaching reading. Although Fries' interest in this problem was aroused by Bloomfield's contribution, he goes far beyond this more superficial work.

The early chapters of Fries (1962) cover in considerable detail the history of reading methods in English (see below 1.1.3), the development of linguistics as a science, a theory of the nature of the reading process based on linguistic considerations, and a careful study of the relationship of English orthography to phonology. Like Bloomfield, Fries objects to the use of phonics on the grounds that trying to connect individual letters with individual sounds proceeding from left to right through the word is confusing to the pupil. Unlike Bloomfield, he considers the basic units of the orthography to be spelling patterns within the word.

He also differs from Bloomfield in his provision for meaningful reading material from the beginning (whereas Bloomfield delayed sentences and stories until after the code-breaking was complete). He also recognized the contrast between content words and function words. (This contrast was already a part of his linguistic study of English — cf. Fries 1940: 108-246; 1952: 87-109.)

A further contribution of Fries was his insistence on teaching by minimal contrast. This included not only the teaching of sets of minimally contrasting words, but also the initial teaching of the alphabet in terms of minimal contrasts.

Fries (1962: 206-7) discusses the importance of intonation as evidence that a pupil has read with understanding (cf. Lefevre 1964). He insists that teachers should not allow oral reading with incorrect intonation to pass. He also stresses, however, that this is not a matter of teaching intonation to the child but rather a matter of using the child's control of intonation as evidence of his understanding.

The next voice in the discussion of the linguistic contribution to reading is that of Carl A. Lefevre (1964), who advocates a sentence method on the grounds that it is impossible to get meaning from the printed page without taking in whole language patterns at the sentence level.

Lefevre includes Fries (1962) in his annotated bibliography, but does not mention him in the text of his book. Whereas Bloomfield and Fries focused on reading as decoding, and the teaching of the phoneme–spelling correspondences, Lefevre focuses on the problem of meaning and begins with sentence structures. In his second chapter, which analyzes the reading problem in America, he sees the reading problem as being not a problem of code breaking but a problem of assigning meaning to linguistic structures larger than a word. He sees the whole of the problem with poor readers and non-readers in high school and college as being a matter of meaning rather than a matter of deciphering the words. It is no surprise, then, that he spends two chapters on sentence structure (one on intonation, the other on sentence patterns), two chapters on word structure, and only one chapter on spelling, word analysis, and phonics. The system of English linguistics which he presents follows the work of Trager - Smith (1951).

Lefevre (1964: 165) also makes a contrast between writing as related to speaking and as heavily dependent on the alphabetic principle, and reading as akin to auding (i.e. listening) — and quite independent of the alphabetic principle. In this same section he argues against phonics, insisting that the pupil should internalize the generalizations for himself beginning from his ability to recognize the larger units and see relationships between them.

Lefevre says of his own method:

What is proposed here is a new sentence method of teaching reading, applying a linguistic description of American English utterances at the sentence level to their graphic counterparts, written and printed sentences. Such a structural linguistic approach to reading and to reading instruction appears very promising, and there is some experimental evidence to support it. (Lefevre 1964: xviii)

In teaching children to read, we should analytically slice larger language segments into smaller ones only to the extent that the learning process requires it. This is the heart of the approach; moving as needed from larger to smaller wholes. (Lefevre 1964: 7)

Another of the important contributions of Lefevre is his view of functors which he calls "structure words". He says

After intonation and sentence order, the most important clues to reading language patterns of sentences are provided by the structure words, or 'empty' words, of American English.

and

[...] first a cautionary note. Structure words, above all, are words that should never be taught in isolation, but always as they function in the language, in typical structural order and patterns. (Lefevre 1964: 119)

There is very little evidence in the education literature that Lefevre's point of view has made any real impact on the teaching of reading in the United States. Most of those who refer to a "linguistic" method are referring to the material of Fries and of Bloomfield and Barnhart.

1.1.3 Continuing debate

From 1963, with the work of Bloomfield, Fries, and Lefevre in print and very much under discussion, the tempo of the debate about methods of teaching reading increased. What is the "best" method? Phonics? Look-say? Some other word or sentence method? Or the "linguistic method"? It is unfortunate that many educators beginning at about this time picked up the word *linguistic* as a sort of charm or talisman and used it with very little understanding of any underlying linguistic principles. This was true both of those who favored the adoption of the Bloomfield or Fries materials, and those who opposed such a change.

Evidence of the wide-spread ferment is seen in the prominence given to the topic of linguistics and reading in various conferences and symposia, and in the education journals. See, for example, the 1965 Annual Conferences on Reading held at the University of Chicago in 1963 and 1965 (Robinson 1963, 1965), the December issue of *The reading teacher* 18 (Stauffer 1964), the December issue of *Elementary English* 42 (cf. Feitelson 1965, Goodman 1965, Pival - Faust 1965, Reed 1965), and *The proceedings of the 13th annual convention of the International Reading Association in 1969* (N.B. Smith 1969). One of the topics in this volume is "Is the linguistic approach an improvement in reading instruction? " (Wardhaugh 1969a, Hughes 1969). For other articles pro and con see Weiss (1963), Betts (1963, 1964), and Bateman - Wetherell (1964).

The excitement about linguistics and reading is also reflected in the publication of two bibliographies on this topic: Broz - Hayes (1966) and Y.M. Goodman - K.S. Goodman (1967).

In 1967, Chall published an excellent discussion of this "great debate" (Chall 1967). She summarizes the "conventional wisdom" of the educators, and the challenges to that conventional wisdom from the linguists, phonic innovations, and the alphabet reformers, especially the i.t.a. (see below 1.2.2). She summarizes all of the research which is available to support one or another of the methods. Unfortunately, it is still the fact that in education most of the research is very poorly conceived, atomistic and unrelated to previous research, and inconclusive.

D. Reed (1970a) provides an elegant analysis, from a linguistic point of view, of the basal series, the language-experience series, the phonic readers, and the linguistic readers.

Once linguistics began to contribute to the methodology of teaching reading in the United States, a number of linguists or linguistically oriented educators made specific suggestions of various kinds. Unfortunately there is not much evidence that most of these have found a way into most of the commercially published materials. The following is a characteristic but not exhaustive list.

Strickland (1963) summarizes the contributions of Bloomfield, Fries, and Smith. She then lists some six ways in which she feels that a linguist can contribute to the teaching of reading, balanced by another dozen ways in which teachers of English, linguistics, and education can contribute. Her suggestion for specific linguistic contributions include: (1) helping the teacher to understand language in general; (2) providing a definitive list of the phonemes of the English language; (3) providing a suggested order for the introduction of grapheme-phoneme correspondences based on frequency of use and utility; (4) providing a suggested order for teaching the reading of the syntactic structures of English as well as the suprasegmentals of pitch, stress, and juncture; (5) providing a definitive list of the spelling patterns used in writing English; (6) helping the teachers to understand the new grammars in contrast to the grammars they have learned in their own schooling.

Allen (1964) focuses on grammatical relationships in the reading material. He is particularly concerned with the contrastive junctures in phrases and included phrases.

Pival - Faust (1965) are concerned about the inadequate word-by-word reading which results from learning words in isolation. They focus on phrases and shifting stress when words occur in normal phrases. They expect that increased attention to phrases in reading might avoid eye-span problems.

Dechant (1969) develops *linguistic phonics* which appears to be simply another phonics method which takes into account some of the material from Bloomfield and Fries on the sound-phoneme relationships.

Gibson (1965) describes the various component elements of learning to read, and proposes a program of theoretical analysis and experiment which is prerequisite to a consideration of formal instruction.

Abercrombie (1963) provides a very useful contrast between spoken monologue and material which is read aloud on the one hand, and conversation on the other. He points out that although we are quite accustomed to hearing spoken prose we are not accustomed to seeing written conversation. This material should be of considerable importance to the teacher of reading – especially as he is considering the styles of language which are familiar to his illiterate pupils.

Gleason (1965), in a discussion of English grammar, presents material that is relevant to the teaching of reading. This includes the discussion of oral language versus written language; the importance of intonation, illustrated by examples from various kinds of reading strategies; a discussion of function words; and a discussion of ambiguity which includes the use of the cloze process – and discusses reading as being essentially like solving a cloze problem.

Wardhaugh (1969c) provides a sharp criticism of both phonics and "reading for meaning" from the point of view of linguistic fact. He concludes with the list of contributions that linguistics might make to the teaching of reading. A later article (Wardhaugh 1971a) points out the difference between linguistics and phonics. It exposes the foolishness of many phonics rules: e.g. the rules for syllabification of *robot* and *robin* which make it obvious that the rules will not work unless the reader already knows what the word is.

Ives (1970) provides another generalized overview of linguistics and reading from a linguist's point of view. He points out as do many of the others that a linguist is not equipped to make decisions about pedagogy or the development of materials. He makes some very low-keyed suggestions as to what the role of the linguist might be.

Mountain (1971) is another attempt to apply intonation to the teaching of reading. He is the victim of a major fallacy, however, in that he is teaching rules in a manner very like phonics.

One final commentary on this phase of the linguistic contributions to the teaching of reading is in the form of a popularized article by Sebasta "My son, the linguist and reader" (Sebasta 1968). Describing his own son's progress in learning to read at home, he notes that in the reading proces as in the speaking process, language is all one piece. He finds that learning cannot ignore meaning or comprehension. He also notes that most adult problems with reading are not primarily a matter of decoding but of understanding.

Who can defend the premise that decoding instruction begins with sound-to-letter relationship exclusive of syntax? The linguist can't tell us this. He's been demonstrating admirably that language, especially *our* language, comes in whole cloth, its distinguishable patterns deriving *not* essentially from single sounds or single words but from utterances and sentence patterns. By whose logic is my son expected to begin his reading task with the smallest units, the threads instead of the patterns? Is he also going to study North America by 'learning' one square mile at a time? (Sebasta 1968: 234)

Wardhaugh and Singer provide a connecting link between some of the earlier work of linguists in the teaching of reading and the newer perspective from psycholinguistics to be examined below in section 1.2. Wardhaugh (1969b) summarizes and discusses the contributions of Bloomfield, Fries, Lefevre, etc. He then characterizes the linguistic theory on which these contributions were based and contrasts it with the TG model. He discusses linguistic insights into reading instruction from the point of view of information processing. He lists six insights that the linguist can offer to the reading teacher or reading researcher. He points out, however, that these insights are linguistic in nature rather than pedagogical. In his chapter "Reading: a new perspective" he recommends that teachers be eclectic rather than stereotyped, pointing out that language has many different facets and that there is no one royal road to learning.

Singer's "Theories, models, and strategies for learning to read" (Singer 1971) includes a section on the linguistic models for reading instruction. He summarizes them as occupying a continuum from decoding to meaning. He places Bloomfield and Fries at the decoding end, and Goodman (1968a) and Ruddell (1970) at the meaning end of the continuum.

1.2 PSYCHOLINGUISTICS AND LITERACY

The newest contributions to literacy come not from descriptive linguistics as such, but from psycholinguistics (a marriage of psychology and linguistics). Although the discipline of psycholinguistics did not develop much until the 1950's and 60's, it is prefigured in the work of Sapir on the psychological reality of linguistic units and the psychological patterning of language (Sapir 1949). Pike, following Sapir, also focused on native reaction and psychological reality in linguistics (Pike 1947, 1967). For another study in this tradition, see Gudschinsky (1958).

For thumbnail sketches of linguistics in psychology, and psychology in linguistics and the beginning of the science of psycholinguistics, see Carroll (1953: 69-111). This early development of psycholinguistics does not relate directly to the teaching of reading. Problems of written communication and the reading process, etc. are absent not only from Carroll (1953) and Miller (1951), but also from Saporta's *Psycholinguistics* (Saporta 1961) and even Osgood - Sebeok (1964), in which the survey of psycholinguistic problems is brought up to date, and in the more recent work by Brown (1970). There was, however, considerable attention to language acquisition, speech perception, and bilingualism which are basic to some of the more recent developments in psycholinguistics applied to literacy.

Miller (1965) is one of the first of the psychologists to begin applying Chomsky's transformational-generative model of linguistics to his psychological experimentation. He lists "seven aspects of human language that should be clearly understood by any psychologist who plans to embark on explanatory ventures in psycholinguistics." (Miller 1965; quoted from the reprint in F. Smith 1973a: 11).

1.2.1 Models of the reading process

Probably the major contribution of psycholinguistics is the development of a number of models of the reading process. These models make it possible to discuss differences of opinion concerning the way children read — or the way they learn to read — in terms of clear-cut theoretical bases.

The model-makers are divided into opposing camps which differ as to the basic nature of the reading process: is it a "psycholinguistic guessing game" in which minimal visual clues are used to confirm hypotheses as to meaning? Or is it an item-by-item linear decoding from written symbol to oral symbol to meaning? (The possibility that it is a different process for different people has not yet entered the discussion. And the obvious fact that the problem for the beginner differs from the problem for the expert is only occasionally taken into account.) The group that views reading as a constructive process include K.S. Goodman and Y.M. Goodman, Ruddell, F. Smith, Kolers, Ryan, Holmes, Venezky and Calfee, and Shankweiler. The other point of view is held by Weaver and Kingston, E. Brown, Gough, and Carroll (see especially Carroll 1964). Entwisle, however, discusses the existence of different cognitive styles in different social and ethnic groups — and the possibility that one model may not be sufficient for all of these.

Goodman's materials derive from a study of miscues in the reading of school children (cf. K.S. Goodman 1967, 1968b, 1969a, 1971, 1972; Y.M. Goodman 1972.)

Ruddell's competence model (Ruddell 1969; and Ruddell - Bacon 1972) is an attempt to pull together various aspects of what is known about the process of reading, including the decoding process, through: grapheme-phoneme correspondences; morphographemic-morphophonemic correspondences; comprehension including relational meaning in both surface structure and deep structure, and lexical meaning; and also the affective and cognitive dimensions.

Frank Smith (1971, 1973) is also developing a model of the reading process. Like K.S. Goodman and Ruddell he sees the reader as predicting his way through a passage of text, eliminating some alternatives in advance on the basis of his knowledge of the redundancy of the language, and acquiring just enough visual information to eliminate the alternatives remaining. Smith's two books and their bibliographies are an excellent starting place for a beginner who wishes to develop enough background in psychology as well as linguistics to understand the discussion of models of the reading process developed by psycholinguists.

The reader should be alert to the fact that all three of these men are reacting strongly against the notion that reading is primarily a decoding process, or that the linguistic contribution to the teaching of reading is limited to the phoneme-grapheme correspondences. Because they are reacting they tend to over-react, and to lose sight of the fact that the ability to focus on specific individual words when necessary is also essential to the reading process, as is the ability to figure out words that have never been seen in print before.

It is interesting to note the background of the three men: K.S. Goodman and Ruddell are both educators with some background in linguistics, and F. Smith is a writer and editor turned linguist and psychologist.

Another researcher who is developing the notion that reading is a clue-search and information-extracting activity is Kolers (1968, 1969, 1970). He has done experiments with text which has been permuted (i.e. reversed, turned upside down, etc.), or is a mixture of more than one language. His experiments demonstrate that reading is not an orderly left-to-right process. It is also evident from his materials that problems of reversals in reading individual letters or words disappear when the reader is reading for meaning within the total context.

For other writers following this same general point of view see Ryan (1969), and F. Smith - Holmes (1971). Smith and Holmes demonstrate that letters, words, and meaning are identified independently of each other. It is clear from their research that the reader uses some notion of the meaning in order to identify words, rather than the identifying of individual words in order to derive the meaning.

A rather different point of view is represented by Weaver - Kingston (1972). It is a preliminary attempt to suggest a model based on the relationship of oral language to reading in the form of fourteen suggested propositions. The point of overlap between oral language and reading is that both use the same "concept storage", and begin from a notion of oral and written signs.

Another recent model of the reading process, based upon adult performance is E. Brown (1970). He summarizes his material as follows:

[...] a model of the reading process in relation to recent research in psycholinguistics. In particular the work of both Lenneberg and Chomsky is reviewed and the parallel is drawn that the inadequacy of learning theory in explaining oral language development may also be true of its application to reading. The model is a portrait of adult reading competence based upon adequate oral language development and focuses on the integration of certain psychological and linguistic mechanisms. It is suggested that analysis-by-synthesis processing of articulatory coding provides considerable insight into how children begin to read. Specifically an acceptable oral rendering is recognized as a significant linguistic event preliminary to further processing. (Brown 1970: 49).

Venezky - Calfee (1970) present a model of the reading process of a competent reader. They consider central to the reading process high-speed visual scanning, dual processing, and the search for the largest manageable unit. The model seems to be most closely related to linguistics as such in the search for the largest manageable unit. This involves "chunking" the material and tagging it for later processing. In regard to this aspect of the model, Venezky and Calfee raise the following questions (among others):

What units are recognized in forward searching?
    How do these units relate to syntax as specified by various grammatical theories?
    What components of unfamiliar words or phrases are recalled when complete recognition is not possible? " (Venezky - Calfee 1970: 285).

One cannot close this section, with its heavy emphasis on reading for meaning without mentioning at least an article or two which present the opposite point of view.

Gough (1972) presents evidence that the reading process does indeed move letter by letter from left to right across the page. He gives his reasons for not agreeing with the people who think that the research results of various sorts would make such a model impossible. He provides a flow chart of his model.

Shankweiler - Liberman (1972) also reject the notion that poor reading in the primary grades results from failure to process material for meaning. (Note that this cause of failure is implicit in the models which assume that reading is a process of hypothesis verification.) They believe that the commonest source of reading failure and disability is the inability to read individual words, and they therefore tested ability to read isolated words in lists, seeking for the causes of failure. They compared their results with the results of tests requiring listening and repetition; and found that the kinds of failure are quite different. Among other results they discovered that reversals (of letters or of words) is a common error in reading words in a list.

John Carroll's view of the reading process (1964, 1970, 1973) is in sharp contrast to the other models that we have considered. He states that reading is less complex than it appears to be and he considers reading to be the understanding of written material in the same way that spoken material is understood.

The activity of reading can, therefore, be analyzed into two processes: (a) on the basis of the written message, the construction or reconstruction of a spoken message or of some internal representation of it; and (b) the comprehension of messages so constructed. It is of the greatest importance to consider these processes separately, even though typically they may occur virtually simultaneously, for different psychological and linguistic problems are involved in each of them. (Carroll 1964: 338).

He sees all of the relationships in the process as stimulus-response since his theoretical base is behavioral psychology.

Entwisle (1971) discusses the implications of language socialization for reading models and for learning to read. She notes that there are divergent cognitive styles in different social and ethnic groups, and hypothesizes that as a result there may not be a *single* model of the reading process which is equally true of all readers; but that there may be a variety of reading processes depending upon the sociolinguistic background of the reader.

Athey (1971a) describes a number of language acquisition models, and discusses their implications for reading. The two developed models of the reading process as such included in her paper are those of Kenneth S. Goodman and Robert B. Ruddell.

1.2.2 Phonology and English orthography

The debate among the proponents of "linguistic" methods or phonic methods and the entrenched proponents of "look-say" methods has inevitably involved the nature of English orthography. This discussion among educators coincided with considerable interest in orthography on the part of the transformational-generative (TG) linguists. This school of linguistics insists on the relevance of underlying forms, in contrast to the structuralists' focus on phonemes. The linguistic description underlying the transformational-generative view of the English orthography is found in Chomsky - Halle (1968), Venezky (1967, 1970a, 1970b, 1970c), and Weir - Venezky (1968). Venezky (1970c) is a complete investigation of English orthography using a computer so that he could examine the problem exhaustively. He accounts for all of the spelling patterns in terms of the TG view of the sound system.

Applications of this view of English orthography to problems of reading are found in Venezky (1970b) and C. Chomsky (1970). The argument is that for the reader the traditional English orthography is optimal, although it provides difficulties for the writer who has to remember some relatively arbitrary spelling rules. The argument for being "optimal" for the reader rests upon notions such as: (a) that the vowel change rules which are used to account for pairs like *courage-courageous, anxious-anxiety, photograph-photography-photographic, sane-sanity*, etc. are regular and productive and a part of what the reader brings with him to reading; and (b) that reading is facilitated by an orthography in which each morpheme is kept in the same shape in all of its occurrences. Carol Chomsky's own article (C. Chomsky 1970), however, provides strong evidence that the orthography is not optimal for the beginning reader (especially, for the small child in an American first grade) who tends to expect the spelling to represent the sounds of his language, and who does not yet control the morphophonemic alternations which are the basis for considering the orthography optimal. One of her suggestions for remedying this situation is to teach the children the forms derived from Latin and the relationship between the members of groups of words such as *bomb-bombardier* etc. This implies that becoming literate requires not just the first year or two of school, with code breaking and practice, but a much lengthier process including the development of control of the learned vocabulary of the language. Steinberg (1973), however, presents evidence that the vowel shift rules, and the awareness of relationship in many sets of words is not present in more than about 10 per cent of university psychology students chosen at random. Clearly even for adults the English orthography is far from optimal.

On the other hand, Klima (1972) suggests that an optimal orthography would have *minimum* redundancy.

A quite different point of view is held by a groups of researchers who find that many people are unable to isolate phonemes in their own speech, and seem to react to syllables more easily. Some of this research seems to have overlooked the fact that in normal naive speech the speaker reacts to phonemes as points of contrast within pronounceable units. He does not normally isolate them in his own speech, and may very well, therefore, fail to recognize them as isolatable units. Among those who find a syllable easier to work with than an individual phoneme, and who recommend teaching by "syllabary" rather than "phonics" or "linguistic" methods are Gleitman - Rozin (1973). Rozin is a psychologist most of whose work was done in the areas of specific hungers and the comparative psychology of learning. Gleitman is a linguist most of whose research has been in the areas of linguistic theory and language acquisition. It would seem that what drove them in the direction of teaching by means of a syllabary is the notion — derived from phonics — that the teaching must be in terms of isolated units which are to be pronounced in isolation and then blended. It is quite clear both from their experimental data and from common-sense expectation that syllables are easier to pronounce in isolation and to blend than individual phonemes. A little more focus on the nature of language might have led them to realize the fallacy of the whole notion of blending.

Others who have worked on the problem of whether or not people can identify phonemes as easily as syllables are Warren (1971), Savin - Bever (1970), and D.L. Brown (1971). At least three articles go so far as to suggest that the reading of logographs would be easier than reading an alphabetic system: Rozin - Poritsky - Sotsky (1971), Gleitman - Rozin (1973), F. Smith (1973b).

A third point of view with regard to orthography is the use in elementary reading of an "initial teaching alphabet" normally referred to as *i.t.a.* This is a semi-phonemic orthography developed by Pitman. The history of the development and use of i.t.a. in teaching beginning readers both in Great Britain and in the U.S., together with arguments for and against its use and a bibliography of primary documents, is found in Dawson (1969), Downing (1969), and Gillooly (1969). The development of i.t.a. seems to be in keeping with the work of one of the earliest proponents of orthography reform, Hart (1551). It is amazing how much his comments, of more than 400 years ago, are still relevant.

Still another point of view on English orthography relates to the differences between oral and written language, including the notion that writing is not a direct representation of speech, but a representation of a style which, although it may be read aloud, is not normal for speaking. Marquardt (1964) points out that children who are learning to read must learn new patterns. He quotes Abercrombie (1963) on the difference between written and spoken language. Reed (1965) uses this as evidence for the point of view that the sequencing in the teaching of reading should be in terms of rules for equating spelling with the spoken representation of English morphemes. (He does not, however, suggest that the rules as such should be taught to the learner.) Various articles pro and con on the hypothesis that written language is "just speech written down" may be found in Levin - Williams (1970). Carterette - Jones (1968) is a research study of phoneme and letter patterns in children's language.

Other aspects of orthography as a complete system may be seen in Gudschinsky (1972), in which she argues that in any orthography, but especially in English, grammatical and lexical features are symbolized as well as phonological features. She gives examples that demonstrate these complex relationships at various levels of linguistic structure.

Holden - MacGinitie (1972) discusses the problem of word boundaries as they are represented in the written language in contrast to children's segmentation of both oral and written language. It is of interest that particularly in the case of functors the children's perception differs from the orthography.

1.2.3 Grammar and literacy

A number of studies relating grammar to the reading process in various ways are grouped together here.

Tatham, Reed, and Jones and Carterette are interested in the relationship between oral language and reading.

Tatham (1970) tests reading comprehension of materials with controlled grammatical patterns. She demonstrates that children understand the patterns that are frequent in their own oral production better than those that are infrequent. She also points out that second graders do not understand clearly the relationship of oral to written language; a full understanding of this relationship seems to develop between grades 2 and 4.

Reed (1970b) suggests that the problem with word-readers (those who read each word individually in a listing intonation pattern) is their failure to see the "linguistic forms" (the lexical and grammatical "formatives"). It does not help such children to say that they should read the way they talk; this is precisely what they cannot do as they do not know what the linguistic forms are. Nor does it help to tell them to "think what the words mean as you read" since they cannot do this until they can perceive the linguistic forms. In illustration he gives a detailed discussion of how questions are recognized both in speech and in reading.

Carterette - Jones (1965) report research on redundancy in oral and written language, and the effects of redundancy on recognition. They found oral and written material to be very different in degree of redundancy, and that the cues involved in visual and auditory recognition are different. They also found differences in the constraints on the occurrence of phonemes or letters in child language and adult language. The same authors (Carterette - Jones 1968) report studies that relate redundancy and linguistic constraints to the amount of information that language conveys, and the ability of the reader to predict sequential elements in reading. They limited this study to constraints on strings of phonemes in oral speech and strings of letters in written material. They gathered and processed by computer a very large amount of both spoken and written material from both children and adults. They found that the constraints on the occurrence of phonemes or letters in the string differed between spoken language and written language, and also differed between child language and adult language.

One observation that is especially useful for making literacy materials comes from their finding that the story *The emperor's new clothes* is easy to read.

But the astonishing thing about these results is the lack of relation between the redundancy of *The emperor's new clothes* and the mean word and sentence length. This text has the longest mean word length and longest mean sentence length we have ever computed [...] It is apparently quite possible to write fairly easy books using long words and long sentences.

The secret, we believe, in writing easy but interesting books is to use a limited lexicon [...] but not to limit it to the few thousand most frequent words in adult language [...] Although a single first grader's vocabulary is limited to 5,000 words (active vocabulary), the total sample of first graders use all the words the eighth graders use. The ones they use depend on their experience not on their frequency in the adult written language. They can use any word and they can read any word; they just can't handle too many at one time in either area. A book they like tells them about something interesting and uses the necessary lexicon to do so. (Carterette - Jones 1968: 131-34).

Scholes and Soderbergh, in very different studies, both note the relevance of a distinction between functors and contentives. Scholes (1970) studies functors and contentives in the behavior of very small children imitating strings of words. He notes that young children in mimicking tend to retain content words and to delete the function words. He refers to Brown - Bellugi (1964), who hypothesize that children omit functors and retain contentives because they have previously learned the contentives as single words, because contentives are high-information words, or that contentives are generally stressed. Scholes, however, concludes:

[...] it can be hypothesized that the child's differential treatment of function and content words in an imitation task involves the following strategy: (a) The child's goal is to find and retain content items, and (b) he identifies content words primarily on the basis of familiarity of form [...] but also, to a lesser extent, on the basis of a knowledge of semantic structure, which allows him to distinguish propositional nuclei from other words. (Scholes 1970: 170).

Soderbergh (1971) is a linguistic study of a Swedish pre-school child's gradual acquisition of reading ability, with a careful linguistic analysis of what she was doing. The child is reported to have had trouble with functor words in isolation; they were first learned when they were put in linguistic context.

The thesis of K.S. Goodman (1969c) is that morphemes rather than words are a basic unit for reading. Children in general do not have an awareness of words when they start to read, but use morphemes as their basic unit. He suggests that reading teachers should shift from emphasis on word recognition to emphasis on comprehension.

Several authors, including Bormuth, Schlesinger, Kaplan, and Ramanauskas explore the relationship of syntax to literacy.

Bormuth (1968) took passages from literature, history, geography, physical science, and biological science, and labelled them as to readability by the formula developed by Chall - Dale (1948). Then he made them into five sets of cloze tests so that every word in every passage is deleted in one or another of the forms. (In each form the fifth word is deleted.) Administering these tests to school children gave a readability score for every word in every passage. The sentences were analyzed in terms of mean word-depth level, independent clause frequency, and independent clause length. Bormuth concludes that the difficulty of mean word-depth and length of an independent clause are not dependent on the reading ability of the subject, and are therefore effective in ranking the readability of written materials for good readers as well as for poor readers. On the evidence of a relatively large difference observed between the sizes of the correlations obtained in analyzing the independent clause level led him to conclude that the difficulty of an independent clause is strongly influenced by the surrounding text.

Schlesinger (1968) worked with fluent adult readers. His study includes chapters on the psychological reality of the syntactic constituent, the effect of grammatical transformations on decoding and encoding behavior, and the effect of sentence complexity, as defined in the work of Yngve (1960) and Chomsky (1957), on the ease of reading. He provides a bibliography of psycholinguistic research preceeding his study, and suggestions for further research.

Levin - Kaplan (1970) build on the work of Schlesinger. They take as given that reading is a sampling process and work with the eye-voice span (the distance to which the eye is ahead of the voice in oral reading). They demonstrate that readers tend to read by phrases — and that this is increasingly true as the reader is older and more experienced. Faster readers also have longer eye-voice spans than slower readers, but the eye-voice span is sensitive to constraints within sentences. The authors conclude,

In summary, we have suggested that the reader, or listener, continually assigns tentative interpretations to a text or message and checks these interpretations. As the material is grammatically or semantically constrained he is able to formulate correct hypotheses about what will come next. When the prediction is confirmed, the material covered by that prediction can be more easily processed and understood. This model of reading, that is, understanding written material, is in its important aspects applicable also to understanding spoken language. (Levin - Kaplan 1970: 132).

Among the growing number of publications regarding structure larger than a single sentence is Ramanauskas (1972). His conclusions are very tentative since he worked only with retarded subjects. He found that the subjects did better on a cloze test based on natural text than on one based on a random mixture of sentences from two stories. He concludes,

Cloze apparently is sensitive to linguistic constraints operating beyond individual sentences, i.e., over longer segments of written text. (Ramanauskas 1972: 87).

Goodman, Weber, and Biemiller have worked with the graphic, grammatical, and semantic cues that school children use in reading.

The earliest work is that of K.S. Goodman (1967, 1969a) in which he develops a protocol for studying reading miscues. He uses the miscue data as a base for his model of the reading process (see above section 1.2.1).

Weber (1970a, 1970b) also analyzes the nature of reading errors in first grade children. She shows that the children use their knowledge of the grammar of the language to narrow the number of words competing for each specific slot in their reading. She noted that the responses which were grammatically correct were almost always semantically correct as well. (These were substitutions for the word actually printed on the page.)

Biemiller (1970) does work very similar to that of Weber. His material goes beyond hers in that he discovered that children use context clues versus graphic clues in three separate stages: (1) they use context clues as they are beginning to learn to read – perhaps avoiding the more difficult task of paying attention to the graphic clues; (2) in a second stage they shift into increased use of graphic clues and also more errors of non-response. The author's guess is that it is during this period that they are first really beginning to understand the exactness of the relationship between spoken words and written words; (3) in a final phase they use both context and graphic clues.

1.2.4 Language acquisition and literacy

The acquisition of language and the beginning reading pupil's awareness of the language that he speaks are further topics developed by the psycholinguists during the sixties and early seventies. These topics are relevant to the teaching of reading because teaching method depends very heavily on the development of the child's language, and also because there is a widespread belief among the psycholinguists that perhaps the child can and should acquire reading in the same sort of way that he acquires oral speech. The references cited are a scattering of what has been done with no attempt to be exhaustive, and the selection is limited to works which mention the teaching of reading, ignoring the large body of literature on language acquisition which does not consider the reading problem at all but is simply concerned with the way a child learns to speak. R. Brown (1973) is an excellent overview of the research on the early stages of language acquisition.

Many of the reading-specific studies of language acquisition build on the work of Lenneberg (1967). His focus is on the biological base of language development. He points out that children learn to speak as a part of a given stage of physical maturation. This is species specific and the progression of development cannot be speeded up. Speech cannot be taught to children; they learn in the developmental process and not by imitation.

In the rather voluminous literature on language acquisition there are three articles which discuss the process of learning to read, spell, and write – especially without a teacher – as parallel to the acquisition of language. The first of these, Torrey (1969) is a case study of a single subject who learned to read shortly after he learned to talk.

Reading for John seems to have been learned but not to have been taught by anyone who was consciously aware of teaching him. He appears to have asked just the right questions in his own mind about the relation between language and print and thus to have been able to bridge the gap between his own language and the printed form. His case may have some implications for the more general task of teaching and learning reading. (Torrey 1969; quoted from F. Smith 1973: 156).

The second article, Gibson (1970), looks at the child's ability to discriminate letters, beginning from his scribble behavior. It is Gibson's thesis that the child develops a set of distinctive features by which he distinguishes letters and letter groups. She goes from differentiating letters — which she considers a very low-order aspect of reading skill — to decoding the written symbols to speech. She says

I have been especially attracted to the idea that there is a carry-over to reading of unit-forming principles in speech. Clusters of phonemes do map with considerable regularity to clusters of letters. Certain combinations of sounds may begin a word, for instance, and also are spelled congruently in a consistent way in this position. These might be called pronounceable combinations, and it could be that pronounceability forms units for the skilled reader. (Gibson 1970: 140).

She also sees morphological usage as another possible source of units, either carried over from speech or found in orthography.

The third article in this group, Read (1971), derives an understanding of some pre-school children's knowledge of English phonology from their spontaneous spelling of English words. These spellings are based on a system of abstract phonological relations. Read's conclusion is that

[...] we have evidence that at least some children do not attend to statistical associations between spellings and autonomous phonemes, which have been the subject of much research in reading. Rather, the children pair spellings with segments abstractly categorized in terms of a hierarchy of articulatory features. (Read 1971: 33).

The children who were studied were pre-schoolers, some as young as three and a half, most of whom were not yet able to read. The children learned the names of the letters and then used blocks or some other moveable-alphabet toy to spell words. They finally produced written messages of all kinds, including stories, letters, and poems. They developed their own spelling systems which persisted well into the first grade, where they gradually gave way to standard spelling under the influence of formal instruction in reading and writing.

It is significant that in the 20 selected clear cases each child arrived at roughly the same system. Each used some spellings that seemed implausible to his parents and teachers, but which can be explained in terms of hypotheses about the children's implicit organization of English sounds.

There are two articles that discuss the child's control of language when he begins his formal schooling. Ruddell (1970) focuses on the fact that contrary to the claims of some linguists, the child continues to develop his language ability throughout his school career. He makes a special point of the fact that the child's ability to comprehend language precedes and exceeds his ability to produce language. He also focuses on the problem of the child whose language model is non-standard. He recommends certain kinds of research to study development of the child's comprehension and grammatical and lexical performance.

Chapman - Calfee - Venezky (1970) focus on certain language and cognitive skills in kindergartners. These include letter matching, rhyming skills, and the ability to delete initial consonants (e.g. "I say *feel*, you say *eel*").

Wardhaugh and Athey in articles in the *Reading research quarterly* (1971) have contrasting points of view with regard to the relationship between theories of language acquisition and theories of reading. Wardhaugh (1971b) reviews various theories of language acquisition including the behavioristic, nativist, and cognitive. He concludes that all are too narrow to offer much to the understanding of the reading process; the acquisition of reading appears to be very different from the theory of language acquisition.

Athey (1971b) reviews an overlapping set of materials, but she concludes that the difference between the acquisition of language and learning to read may be an artifact of teaching methods which would disappear if teaching methods were changed. She considers that language acquisition may indeed help provide a model for learning to read. It is significant, however, that she looks at language acquisition from the point of view of psychology and cognitive development rather than from the point of view of the linguist who holds that acquisition of language patterns is practically complete by the time a child is five.

We conclude this section with two points of view on language awareness and the teaching of reading. Savin (1972) points out that many non-readers in the early primary school are unaware of phonemes, rhyme, etc. in their own speech. He suggests that syllables be used to teach these children since they have readiness for neither the phonics approach nor the word approach which have been in use for the past hundred and thirty years. (For other suggestions for the use of syllables in the teaching of reading, see below section 3.1).

Mattingly (1972) points out that reading, unlike speaking and listening depends upon *linguistic awareness*. This awareness varies considerably from person to person. He says

> Reading is seen not as a parallel activity in the visual mode to speech perception in the auditory mode; there are differences between the two activities that cannot be explained in terms of the difference of modality. They can be explained only if we regard reading as a deliberately acquired, language-based skill, dependent upon the speaker-hearer's awareness of certain aspects of primary linguistic activity. By virtue of this linguistic awareness, written text initiates the synthetic linguistic process common to both reading and speech, enabling the reader to get the writer's message and so to recognize whatever has been written. (Mattingly 1972: 145).

1.2.5 Aural and visual perception and literacy

There have been a great many studies in perception as related to the reading process, a number of them with a linguistic component. I quote here only a few of these studies, but each of these includes a bibliography which the interested reader can use to broaden his search for material on this topic.

Jones (1968) reviews the body of literature on the perceptual units used in language processing, and concludes that words and sentences are not really the units through which spoken language is perceived. This, of course, casts doubt upon much of the work that has been done in teaching reading which is built around the word: controlled vocabulary, sight vocabulary, word attack skills, etc. Jones' conclusion is that something should be done to bridge the gap between the cues used for oral perception by six-year-old speakers of English and the cues available in the reading material from which they are learning to read. Her suggestions include the underlining of words which are to be read as one unit, the indication of primary stress by red type or red underlining, and the indication of crucial pitch changes by a light blue line behind the line of type.

Hansen - Rodgers (1968) conclude that the crucial psycholinguistic units in initial reading are letter sequences smaller than a word.

Kolers (1968a) experimented with the perception of text which had been transformed in various ways (e.g. whole sentences into mirror images, whole sentences upside down, individual letters in mirror image or upside down, etc.). His findings suggest the need for a reconsideration of much that is done in reading instruction based on a simpler model of visual perception in reading. Kolers himself says,

> We have wanted to study something about the acquisition of skill with such materials which, because of their unfamiliarity, magnify the reading process somewhat; and we have been interested also in the topic of adaptation to geometric distortion. Our aim, as

we continue experiments of this kind, is to find out how the skilled reader extracts information from the little black marks on a page, and to learn more about the nature of the interplay between skilled movement and information processing. What we have found so far does not even establish the limits of the field of study. (Kolers 1968a:40).

Smith - Holmes (1971: 394) examine and reject the following traditional assumptions about fluent reading:

That identification of letters is a necessary preliminary to word identification, and that an identification of words is a prerequisite for comprehension.

They propose a "feature analytic model" in which letter identification, word identification, and the comprehension of meaning are to be distinct tasks that can be performed independently on the same visual information.

Crowder (1972) represents another line of research in the relationship between visual and auditory memory.

In an earlier article, Gibson - Pick - Osser - Hammond (1962) survey the literature on the critical unit of language for the reading process. Their earliest bibliographical entries are from the twenties, and there is a fairly large body of material from the fifties. This article, however, moves away from earlier work on the orthographic words or the letter of the orthography to a unit which constitutes the relationship between the phoneme of the spoken language and the spelling patterns of the written language — the grapheme-phoneme correspondence. They conclude that

[...] the perceptual process has been facilitated in skilled readers for units discovered during long exposures to the grapheme-phoneme correspondences of the English language. (Gibson - Pick - Osser - Hammond 1962: 570).

In the rapidly expanding literature on psycholinguistics, bibliographies are quickly outmoded. However, anyone interested in the earlier developments in psycholinguistics and the teaching of reading will find the small annotated bibliography *Linguistics, psycholinguistics, and teaching of reading* (Y.M. Goodman - K.S. Goodman 1971) very useful. The bibliography includes some 163 items in chapters on linguistics and language study; comprehension, semantics, and meaning; curriculum; dialects and related problems; general application of linguistics and psycholinguistics to reading; instruction in reading; intonation; relationship between oral and written language; research; syntax and grammar; the reading teacher and linguistics; theories of reading; and word recognition.

1.3 SOCIOLINGUISTICS: BILINGUAL AND DIALECT EDUCATION

The civil rights and ethnic minorities movements of the 50's and 60's led, in the United States, to a new focus on language problems in literacy in the elementary school. The "Bilingual Education Act" (Title VII) of January 2, 1968, provided funds for the development of bilingual programs and was therefore a direct stimulus to the study of problems of language interference in literacy. At the same time, intensified ethnic consciousness among the American Indians led to a new focus on the Indian languages in the educational programs of the Bureau of Indian Affairs. Furthermore, the civil rights movements led to new attention to black dialect, and its relationship to literacy in the inner-city, predominantly black, population. In all of these new interests there was some involvement of linguists. Unfortunately, that involvement has been much less than ideal and some programs have developed with small attention to the linguistic problems involved.

Andersson - Boyer (1970) provides an extensive discussion of bilingual education in the United States including the history of minority languages in the United States, the rationale for bilingual schooling, suggested directions for action and research, and the implications of bilingual schooling for education and society. In appendices it also outlines the history of various language groups within the United States. Although it makes little mention of the linguistic contributions to these problems, it does set the social and political stage for such investigations. The bibliography includes material on the linguistic aspects of bilingualism.

Rosen - Ortego (1969) is an annotated bibliography on the language and reading instruction of Spanish-speaking children. It is significant, however, that a large part of this bibliography concerns general factors such as the measuring of intelligence, reading achievement, and bilingual education in general; only a small part relates directly to the linguistic factor as such, or to the contribution of linguists. It is amazing that very little of an immense amount of research and discussion on the linguistic phenomena of bilingualism, language contact, etc. has had any real impact on the actual teaching of reading in the bilingual education programs under Title VII.

Under Title VII, and as a result of a growing interest in bilingual education on the part of the Bureau of Indian Affairs, there are a number of bilingual education projects for Indian groups in the United States. There is not, however, very much in print with regard to these programs, or with regard to the impact of linguistics on them. Some of them do make use of linguistic consultants. Linguists of the Summer Institute of Linguistics, Inc., are involved in the programs in Crow, Zuni, Mikasuki Seminole, Eskimo, and others. Other linguists are involved in the programs in Cherokee, Crow,

Navajo, and others.

There seems to be more documentation of the Navajo program than the others. The interested reader should consult the serial publications: (a) *Language in American Indian education* (Newsletter of the Office of Education Programs, Bureau of Indian Affairs, United States Department of the Interior; available from the Division of Educational Planning and Development, P.O. Box 1788, Albuquerque, NM 87103) and (b) *Navajo reading study progress reports* (available from the University of New Mexico, Albuquerque, NM).

The larger contribution of linguistic science has been to the special programs for speakers of Black English.

The interested reader will find descriptions of Black English (also called *Negro, non-standard,* or *inner-city*) in Labov *et alii* (1969), Shuy (1969a) and Stewart (1969).

In spite of the growing body of materials on the linguistic analysis of Black English, there is a great deal of disagreement as to how this should apply to the actual teaching of reading in the school system. The discussion revolves not only around the facts concerning Black English itself, but includes controversy on the following parameters: (a) Does being the speaker of a non-standard language make it more difficult for a child to achieve in school? (b) Should a "disadvantaged" child be taught to read his own dialect, or should he be taught "standard" English before learning to read? (c) Should speakers of non-standard dialects be given specially prepared materials, or should the materials for all children reflect the common core of all the dialects? — These parameters are discussed in a series of brief articles in Laffey - Shuy (1973). The advantage of beginning one's reading with this book is that each article includes an extensive and excellent bibliography on each topic.

There seems little question that the speaker of a non-standard dialect has more difficulty in school than the speaker of standard English. There is considerable disagreement, however, as to whether these difficulties stem from linguistic problems or from social problems. Modiano (1973) outlines the various ways that language can interfere with the acquiring of reading skills, including the problem of phoneme identification, the problem of associating sounds with words which are not known, and the problem of getting meaning from a language that the reader does not speak. Weber (1973) provides an analysis of oral reading hazards focusing on the apparent errors of the speakers of non-standard English. Melmed (1973) points out that the phonological interference is much greater in words which are read in lists than in words in proper context. Many pairs of words which are homonyms in Black English but not in standard English give trouble in reading only in isolation.

Other difficulties for the speaker of Black English are found in Labov (1967, 1970), Baratz (1969).

There is pressure on the part of educators to teach standard English to speakers of non-standard dialects, and to use only standard English as a medium of instruction in literacy. There is reaction to this from the linguists who have studied black dialect. In general they recommend that there be some modification of the teaching program in the direction of using black dialect as a medium of instruction, and the acceptance of black dialect in the pupil's responses even when standard English is being used in the reading material. (See K.S. Goodman (1970a), Rystrom (1969, 1970a, 1970b, 1973), Serwer (1969), K.S. Goodman (1965), Fasold (1969), Wolfram - Fasold (1969), Stewart (1969), Leaverton (1973), and Seymour (1973).)

Baratz (1973) provides an excellent review of the research on the relationship of Black English to reading. Further bibliography is available in Hall (1972) and in Fearn - Matucci (1969).

LINGUISTICS AND LITERACY IN THE ETHNIC
LANGUAGES OF THE WORLD

As indicated in the Introduction, the term *ethnic language* is my coinage for the languages which are neither world languages nor the national language of the countries in which they are spoken. The impact of linguistics on literacy in these languages has been quite different from its impact on elementary education in the United States: (1) Linguistic methods in the Bloomfield-Fries tradition have not yet diffused to countries which are using traditional European methods or have adopted U.S. methods current in the forties and fifties. (2) Psycholinguistic investigation of the reading process has been restricted to world languages; no one knows whether or not the findings are applicable to the ethnic languages. (3) UNESCO, the largest promotor of literacy in the developing nations, is promoting 'functional literacy' (the marriage of literacy to community development projects) and ignoring linguistic and pedagogical considerations.

This section reflects the fact that the major input from linguistics has been in three areas: sociolinguistic considerations of language policy, including the choice of instructional medium (see below section 2.1), the construction and revision of orthographies (section 2.2), and a minor contribution to literacy method (section 2.3).

2.1 SOCIOLINGUISTICS, LANGUAGE POLICY,
AND LITERACY

A majority of the world's nations have the problem of multilingualism. There are distinct ethnic groups using their own languages — either unabsorbed immigrant communities, or indigenous populations. In the case of the newer nations, one of the first problems has been what to choose as a national language: One of the indigenous languages? An indigenous-based lingua franca? Or a world language?

But the choice of a national language does not end the linguistic problems. What shall be the medium of instruction in the country's schools? Shall school children be allowed to begin their education in their mother tongue? Or shall they begin in a semi-familiar lingua franca or regional language? Or must they from the beginning make use of a world language? If they begin in the mother tongue, how long should instruction in this language continue? How will transition be made into a second language? If, on the other hand, the choice is made to begin instruction in a language which is not the pupil's mother tongue, how are they to learn that language?

And what of adult education? Are adult literacy programs to be carried out in the mother tongue of the learner? Or is he to be taught directly in a second language?

And what will bilingualism (or multi-lingualism) do to the community? Can people control two languages equally? What will they be able to do in their dominant language? Or in their weaker language?

Increasingly since World War II questions of this sort have been in focus both on a practical level and for linguistic and anthropological theoreticians in the growing science of sociolinguistics. There is, of course, a long history of shifting government policy in various places with regard to these matters. See, for example, Heath (1972) for the history of language policy in Mexico, and Andersson - Boyer (1970) for a discussion of language policy in the United States.

Pronouncements about the use of the mother tongue for educational purposes — especially during the first three years of primary school — have been made from time to time. See Benzies (1940) for a declaration made in Rome in 1930 with regard to the use of the mother tongue in Africa. UNESCO (1953) contains one of the most important statements concerning the use of the vernacular in education worldwide. It is this statement which is used as a base for decisions in many countries. Downing (1973) discusses the problem of match or mismatch of the child's language with the language of instruction in reading in the fourteen countries where he surveyed the teaching of reading and its relationship to language.

The rest of the references on this topic are organized by geographical areas, although some of the content is actually of a more general nature.

There are a number of exellent references on sociolinguistics and literacy in Africa. The very extensive article of Foster (1971) deals with the problems of literacy in Sub-Saharan Africa. Whitely (1971) is a collection of papers presented and discussed at the Ninth International African Seminar held in Dar-es-Salaam in 1968. It includes a section of general and theoretical studies on such topics as national languages and languages of wider communication in developing nations, the roles of languages in multilingual societies, a social psychology of bilingualism, cognitive aspects of bilingual communication, etc. Other sections deal with the implications and results of particular language policies, varieties of education and language policies including the implications of a choice of medium of instruction, and contrasting patterns of literacy acquisition in a multilingual nation.

There is by no means complete agreement as to the advantage of using the mother tongue in Africa, however. The pros and cons are surveyed in Berry (1952). Dames (1965) argues in favor of the use of the mother tongue in Kenya, while Kehoe (1963) argues against the use of the mother tongue and in favor of the choice of English from the beginning in Ethiopia. These are representative of a large number of articles on this subject.

Lastra (1968) provides an excellent survey of literacy in Latin America, including the problem of the Indian languages alongside Spanish and Portuguese. This can be supplemented by articles on specific countries and situations: Nida (1949) discusses the language policy of Mexico and advocates the use of diglot materials. Wallis (1956) discusses the sociolinguistic problems in Mesquital Otomi (Mexico) transition education. Garvin (1954) discusses a specific problem of language and culture as it impinges on literacy. Bilingual schools in Peru for the jungle Indians, and later for the Highland Quechua, are discussed together with the social and cultural implications in a series of articles: Best (1961), Burns (1971), Wise (1971), and Shell (1971).

A series of articles relate language policy, language engineering, and literacy in Oceania – New Guinea and Australia: Wurm (1971); the Philippines: Sibayan (1971); the trust territory of the Pacific islands: Trifonovitch (1971); Indonesia and Malaysia: Alisjahbana (1971); and French Polynesia: Lavondes (1971).

In addition to these general articles the following provide a sampling of specific material from the various regions.

From Australia recommendations for education for the Aborigines are found in Harris (1968) and Watts (1971). A discussion of language and literacy in Papua New Guinea is found in Wurm (1966).

Materials from the Philippines include a discussion of the role of the various languages in Philippine education (Hunt 1966) and the report of experiments in education through the vernacular: Davis (1967), and Orata (1953).

Leibowitz (1971) discusses a history of the use of English in American Indian schools in the United States including destructive government policies and their relationship to economic and political problems.

Coombs (1971) reports rather surprising but non-conclusive evidence that children presently in a BIA bording school at Chinle seem to do as well in their school work as the children at the Rough Rock and Rock Point schools which are fully bilingual in Navajo.

Bauer (1971) gives a brief history of bilingual education in the Bureau of

Indian Affairs schools.

There are some sources that either argue against the use of the mother tongue in education, or ignore the language problem entirely.

As late as 1956 Fairchild as consultant to the Royal Afghan Ministry of Education could discuss religion, attitudes, indigenous culture, etc. as essential to a literacy program without even mentioning the language or linguistic problems (cf. Fairchild - Wann 1956).

The opinion that direct teaching of the second language is *more* effective than teaching people to read through their own language — is espoused by Borja (1958).

In Stevens' report on the national mass-literacy program of the government of Mali (Stevens 1963) the only mention of language is a list of the various local languages with the number of speakers of each and the indication that there is no literacy in any of these languages.

2.2 ORTHOGRAPHIES: CONSTRUCTION AND REVISION

A large number of ethnic languages have been written and used for literacy teaching for the first time during the past 4 or 5 decades. The major considerations in devising or revising orthographies for such languages are social and practical, as well as linguistic. It is in this field that linguistics in general has made its greatest impact on literacy in the underdeveloped nations.

An excellent summary of the problems of orthography formation or revision, with criteria for the decisions, is found in Smalley (1964). This volume also includes a bibliography for the interested reader.

Among the linguists interested in problems of orthography preparation there is general agreement that an ideal orthography is basically phonemic with a single representation for each phoneme of the language. This representation may be a single symbol, a letter plus diacritics, or a digraph or trigraph. There is, however, disagreement as to the extent that morphemes should be spelled the same way in all occurrences (e.g. the -*s* plural of *dogs* and *cats*). For early treatments of the linguistic problems from the point of view of phonemics see Nida (1947) and Pike (1947).

There is a great deal of disagreement about some elements even in a relatively phonemic orthography. Linguists differ as to whether suprasegmental phonemes such as tone, stress, nasalization, and the like should always be written. A sample of the extensive material on this topic can be found in Powlison (1968) and Gudschinsky's critical review thereof (Gudschinsky 1970a); see also Gudschinsky (1959b).

The relationship of psycholinguistic testing and orthography is discussed in Gudschinsky - Popovich - Popovich (1970). In the Maxakali language a test which involved teaching a speaker of the language to read and build words from lettercards was used to verify a highly unusual phonemic analysis. This analysis, in turn, was used as the base for an orthography which proved very teachable in a literacy program for Maxakali speakers.

Interesting sidelights on non-Roman orthographies, and their implications for literacy merit some mention. Butt (1967) bases a teaching method for Hindi specifically on the major orthographic problem in the Devanagari script. In that script the central schwa vowel is not indicated in syllables which begin with a consonant. This lack of symbolization greatly complicates the problem of teaching reading.

A quite different sort of orthographic problem is found in Walker (1969). He discusses the syllabaries which were developed for American Indian languages and their relationship to literacy in these languages. He includes Sequoyah's syllabary for Cherokee and Evans' syllabary for Cree.

There has been only a small amount of focus on the fact that an orthography consists of far more than a list of letters to represent phonemes. The most inclusive discussion of this – including representation of the phonology, of grammar, and of lexicon, at all levels of their respective hierarchies – is found in Gudschinsky's "Linguistics and literacy" (Gudschinsky 1974). Typical treatments of specific problems such as word division are found in Wolff (1954) and Bergman (1971).

The sociolinguistic problems of orthography making can be very severe. One of the best illustrations of the cultural and emotional problems involved is found in Tucker (1952). Another specific example in the setting of Latin America is found in Burns (1953). Sjoberg (1966) gives a more general survey of the kinds of modifications suffered by phonemic alphabets as a result of social and political pressures.

Of special interest as a synthesis of linguistic and social considerations in orthography making is Tucker's history of orthographic systems in SUB-Saharan Africa (Tucker 1971).

The vexing questions of the relationship of orthography to reading is explored by Downing (1972) by comparing literacy acquisition in differing cultures and languages with the aim of discovering the universal psycholinguistic processes of learning to read and write which may be revealed by such contrasts. Data were collected in fourteen countries: Argentina, Denmark, Finland, France, Germany, Great Britain, Hong Kong, Israel, India, Japan, Norway, Sweden, USA, and USSR. The contrasting orthographies in this list include the logographic system of Chinese and the syllabic kana system of Japanese as well as various alphabetic systems.

2.3 METHODS OF TEACHING LITERACY

2.3.1 Traditional methods

It has been common practice in most countries to teach the ethnic minorities in the national language of the country. Even where the ethnic language is used in primary education, it is usual to pattern the books and teaching methods on those of the dominant language.

It was interest in adult literacy in the ethnic languages that led to the development of two quite different methods in the twenties and thirties, the Laubach syllable method and Townsend's psychophonemic method. Both were attempts to find a simple fast method of learning that could be used everywhere.

World interest in adult literacy was triggered by the work of Frank C. Laubach, which began in the Philippines in 1930. There he developed a key word method in which he derived the forty syllables of the Maranaw language from three long words which together used all of the consonants once and only once in combination with the vowel *a*. In later work, especially in India, Laubach found that other languages did not lend themselves to this particular method. He therefore developed the now well-known "Laubach method" in which pictures are used to serve as keys to words and the words in turn serve as keys to their initial sounds. This method has been used very widely in adult campaigns in India, Africa, and Latin America, without any consideration of the nature of the languages. (See references by Laubach in the bibliography).

The psychophonemic method was originated by W.C. Townsend in the '20's and further developed with the collaboration of his wife E.M. Townsend (Townsend 1948, 1952), for use in Indian languages of Guatemala, Mexico, and Peru. The method consists of recognizing whole words by comparison with each other, and eventually using these words in sentences and stories. It differs from a typical look-say method in that the words are very carefully controlled in terms of letters. A psychophonemic primer begins with from three to five letters, and adds new ones one at a time. It is expected that in the process of comparison and word recognition the pupil will learn to associate the letters with the phonemes they represent. The method is not significantly modified for languages of very diverse structure.

Later versions of the psychophonemic method, especially in Peru, added various kinds of syllable practice and word building. Such exercises were developed because of the observed needs in particular languages, and were to that extent language-specific. They did not, however, fit any particular theory of the relationship of linguistics to reading beyond the sound-symbol relationship.

2.3.2 Linguistic contributions to literacy method

In the ethnic languages there was an early lip service to the notion that literacy pedagogy should be based on adequate linguistic analysis, but the actual application of linguistics to literacy was slow and fragmentary. In the early forties, for example, K.L. Pike demonstrated that the minimal phonological units of Mixtec (an Indian language of Mexico) are disyllabic couplets rather than syllables but this fact was not reflected in teaching method before 1970. (See below section 3).

Beekman (1950) reports an experiment in the use of syllables in the teaching of reading in Chol (an indigenous language of Mexico) based on the primary importance of the syllable in Chol phonological structure. The linguistic input is minimal, however, including only: (a) a sequencing of material in terms of frequency of phonemes, and (b) the use of the predominant syllable pattern as a starting place.

Neijs (1958, 1960) paid attention to the phonemicness of orthography; the use of phoneme-letter correspondence as a unit; the use of phoneme frequency as a criterion in the sequencing of materials; and the use of syllables, words, and sentences as structural units.

Sadler (1959), in materials for literacy campaigns in Africa, made almost no use of linguistic criteria in spite of his linguistic background. He did, of course, encourage the use of phoneme-based orthographies, and paid attention to the frequency of phonemes in the language in planning his sequencing. He used the syllable as the basic unit of teaching which may well be linguistically sound in the kind of languages he was working with.

McCullough (1965) in her material on the preparation of textbooks, which was developed on the basis of her experience in India, shows some concern about the linguistic structure of the language. She recommends that the vocabulary of pupils be used as a base from which the vocabulary of curriculum materials can be developed. She expresses an interest in the morphology, syntax, word clusters, sound sequences, punctuation, and parts of speech. She also tabulates sentence sizes and types. Most of this, however, is based on parallels with English grammar or on the orthography rather than on a solid foundation in modern descriptive linguistics.

The "Creative Reading" method of Larudee (1972) is another application of the phoneme-equals-grapheme principle very reminiscent of phonics. This particular interpretation is based on TG grammar rather than on the older classical phonemics, but it results in very much the same kind of material.

Wallis (1952) describes the use of various kinds of linguistic units in literacy primers made by members of the Summer Institute of Linguistics. It does not appear, however, that the use of syllables, morphemes, words, or sentences reflected any coherent theory of the relationship of linguistics to literacy.

3

A FULLY LINGUISTIC METHOD

So far as I know, the most extensive application of linguistics to problems of literacy is in materials made under my direction by my own method. The development of my method began with work with the Mazatec Indians of Mexico between 1949 and 1955. An early version of it is found in Gudschinsky (1951, 1952). It developed during the years of work with the Mazatec and subsequent work in Brazil. Gudschinsky (1959a) describes the result of those years of experience. By the mid-1960's I was working on a much broader front as International Literacy Coordinator of the Summer Institute of Linguistics, Inc., coordinating and helping to develop literacy programs in some 500 ethnic languages scattered through more than 20 countries, including: Australia, Papua New Guinea, Philippines, South Viet Nam, South America, Mexico, West Africa, and the Indian languages of the United States and Canada. The majority of these languages were unwritten before the beginning of the Institute's work on linguistic investigation, translation, and literacy. In a large number of these languages the Institute has done the first literacy work; in others the Institute serves governments in helping to provide vernacular materials and vernacular teacher training as a part of national bilingual programs. In addition to work with SIL, I spent 6 months at Literacy House, Lucknow, India where I directed the making of literacy primers in 14 different languages, involving 9 different scripts. It was in a workshop in South Viet Nam for the producing of materials for the Highlander Bilingual Education Project that some of the details of the revised method began to come into focus, under the name of "the focused drill method". A discussion of the method as it was at that stage − about 1968 − may be found in Gudschinsky (1973). The method continues to develop, and the following discussion is based on the newest techniques and usage.

In its larger setting, a total literacy program for a pre- or semi-literate community includes the following: stimulation and development of a native-authored literature with ongoing training of authors and outlets for their product; the development of literacy as a community value; a literacy-readiness program for the people of the community and especially of the prospective pupils; the development of a locally supported and motivated organizational structure for the teaching of both adults and children, and for the training of teachers and supervisors to insure an ongoing program; and the preparation of materials for vernacular classes and for transition into the second language (where the social and cultural considerations require that the people become bilingual in the dominant language if they are to enter the main stream of their nation's life). All of this must be done within the constraints both of the local language and culture, and of the national language and culture within which it is embedded.

For the purposes of this brief résumé of the method, however, I will restrict myself to the essential elements of the "primer" or instructional materials for the teaching of reading and writing in the mother tongue, as it is here, perhaps, that linguistic input is most needed. It should be noted in passing that the method presupposes the use of prepared textbooks and materials. This is not to deny the value of pupil-authored materials in the hands of a competent teacher. In many of these almost wholly illiterate or semi-literate communities, however, the teaching must be done by teachers who are themselves barely literate, and it is necessary to begin with prepared materials that these teachers can use with confidence and effectiveness. It is to be hoped that as the teachers develop competence and experience they will be able to develop new materials of their own far better than those prepared for them.

3.1 PEDAGOGICAL OUTLINE

The following outline of my method is exceedingly simplified. It is given here solely for the purpose of indicating the various ways in which linguistic analysis is applied to it. A fuller exposition (possibly sufficient to permit an interested reader to use the method himself) may be found in Gudschinsky (1970b, 1973), and various articles in *Notes on literacy*.

Typically, a lesson in a primer made by this method has four parts: (I) a section which is explicitly teaching the decoding of content words and morphemes ("word-attack skills"); (II) a section which is explicitly teaching a "chunking" of longer utterances into phrases or minimal clauses with the aid of function morphemes recognized at sight in context; (III) a section which practices these skills in the context of connected reading material which is culturally and linguistically adequate; (IV) a section on penmanship, spelling, and creative writing. In many primers, lessons that have a section on decoding alternate with lessons that have a section on chunking. A review lesson may have any combination of these elements.

ad (I): A typical decoding section consists of the following parts (the letters match the parts of the illustrations which follow):

(a) a keyword (or key phrase) labeling the picture which represents it. The keyword is broken down to provide the pronounceable matrix (either syllable or couplet) within which new letters may be substituted, and the nucleus of that unit which can be used as a base for further exercises;

(b) the rebuilding of the pronounceable matrix of the keyword, and the subsequent building of new units which can be made by combining the new letter with letters previously known;

(c) the reading of the new syllables or couplets in vertical array in order to focus on the fact that the new element is the same in appearance and pronounciation in all the units;

(d) the contrast of the new letter with other letters already taught which can occur in the same position;

(e) the use of the new syllables or couplets in the building of new words – using the nucleus of the word as the point from which to build even if the nucleus does not happen to be the first syllable.

Special lessons must be devised for teaching suprasegmental phonemes such as tone, nasalization, stress, length, etc. Other lessons teach familiar symbols in new positions within the syllable or couplet.

The following are several examples from Portuguese of the steps in the decoding section. Everything except the item in focus has been taught in previous lessons.

Example 1 (p- initial in syllable):

(a) *pato* (keyword providing syllable matrix and
     pa   the nucleus *a*.)
     a

(b) *a   i   o   u*   (new syllable building)
     pa pi po pu

(c) *pa*
     pi   (comparison focusing on *p*)
     po
     pu

* (a picture of a duck)

48

(d) | pa | pi | po | pu |
     | va | vi | vo | vu | (contrast of *p* with *v* and *d*)
     | da | di | do | du |

(e) | pa | so | po | pa | pe |
     | pato | sopa | povo | pai | pena | (word building)
     | "duck" | "soup" | "people" | "father" | "sympathy" |

Example 2 (an alternative spelling for nasalized vowel -Vn by analogy with oral vowels):

(a) *
     ponte
     pon   (keyword providing vowel + nasal marker
     on   -*n* as a matrix)
     o

(b) | o | i | e | a |
     | on | in | en | an | (new nasalized vowels built by analogy)

(c) *on*
     in
     en   (comparison focusing on nasal marker)
     an

(d) | on | in | en | an |
     | om | im | em | am | (contrast of -*n* and -*m*)

(e) | on | in | in | en | an |
     | pon | tin | lin | pen | san | (word
     | ponte | tinta | linda | pente | santo | building)
     | "bridge" | "paint, ink" | "beautiful" | "comb" | "saint, holy" |

* (a picture of a bridge)

Example 3 (subordinate -l- in cluster with p, b, c, and g):

*
(a) *planta*   (keyword providing a syllable matrix, and
     plan   the nucleus *pan*)
     pan

(b) *pan   pa   bu   ca   go*   (syllable building)
     plan pla   blu   cla   glo

(c) *plan*
     pla
     blu   (comparison focusing on *l* in clusters)
     cla
     glo

(d) *pla   blu   cla   glo*   (contrast of *l* and *r* in clusters)
     pra   bru   cra   gro

(e) *plan*   *blu*   *cla*   *glo*   *pra*   (word
     planta   *blusa*   *classe*   *globo*   *prato*   building)
     "plant"   "blouse"   "class"   "globe"   "plate"

* (a picture of a plant)

Example 4 (trilled *rr* medial in couplet — never initial in word with this spelling):

*
(a) *garrafa*
     garra   (keyword providing a couplet matrix and
     arra   nucleus)
     a

(b)   *a   o   i   e   o*   (couplet building)
     arra   arro   arri   erra   orra

(c) *arra*
     arro
     arri   (comparison focusing on *rr*)
     erra
     orra

* (a picture of a bottle)

(d) *arra arro erra orro*
  ara   aro   era   oro   (contrast of *rr* with *r* and *nh*)
  anha anho enha onho

(e) *e*   *an*   *o*   *en*
  erra   *arran*   *orro*   *orren*   (word
  terra   *arranca*   *chorro*   *corren*   building)
  "earth"   "pull up"   *cachorro*   *corrente*
                         "dog"   "chain"

ad (II): A typical section for teaching the recognition of the functors includes the following elements (*Functors* are morphemes which belon to the closed classes and whose meaning is primarily grammatical rather than lexical. They may be either words, clitics, or affixes.): (a) a key sentence or sentence sequence from which the functor can be derived (this sequence must be sufficient to trigger the use of the functor); (b) the breakdown of the key sequence to the smallest meaningful chunk which includes the new functor; (c) the building of new phrases or clauses using the new functor; (d) the contrast of the new functors with other functors which occur in the same position, and which have been taught previously.

An example from Portuguese of a functor lesson (contrasting *ao* "to the" used with masculine nouns and *à* "to the" used with femine nouns.):

(a) *Paulo ia ao monte.*   Paul went to the mountain.

(b)   *ao monte.*   to the mountain.

(c)   *campo*   country
          ao campo.   to the country.
    Ele ia ao campo.   *He went* to the country.

(d)   *vila*   village
          à vila.   to the village.
    Ele ia à vila.   He went to the village.

ad (III): The third section of each reading lesson is a story or other connected texts — poetry, conversation, essay, etc. It uses only those things which have already been taught, and is specifically designed to give additional practice in the letters or functors which are new in this particular lesson. The most important requirement for this reading material is that it be both culturally and linguistically natural for the reader. It also should be extensive enough to give adequate practice.

ad (IV): The fourth section of the lesson is the penmanship, spelling, and creative writing lesson. These are combined, since penmanship alone is inadequate for independent writing. The lesson consists of instruction in the formation of new letters, and in figuring out how to spell non-arbitrary patterns; special instruction in the spelling of arbitrary patterns; practice in writing from dictation; and the writing of spontaneous creative material.

3.2 LINGUISTIC BASE

A primer by my method is ideally based on a complete linguistic analysis of the language, including phonology, grammar, and lexicon, and also a thorough analysis of the relationship of the orthography and spelling to the language. It requires input from the linguistic analysis at every point and in much more detail and sophistication than has ordinarily been taken into account in planning primers. It should be noted that even native speakers of the language need input from such a linguistic analysis. In English, for example, a native speaker's control of the language does not prevent the authors of American primers from perpetrating lexical nonsense such as "Run, rat, run! Run to the red sun! "; non-English grammar such as "Oh! Oh! Oh! See Dick run! "; virtually unsayable sequences such as "See Skip, Jane! " or non-stories which are equally story-like (or un-like) whether they are read from the bottom up or the top down.

The linguistic model which underlies the following comments is tagmemics (Longacre 1964, Pike 1967). This has proved to be far more practical for field work and primer making than the more popular transformational-generative model as can be seen from the following outline of tagmemic analysis which relates it to primer making. The model is in a state of rapid development; the following descriptions of phonological, grammatical, and semantic analysis are limited to aspects relevant to literacy, and in no way represent the full range of tagmemic theory and research.

Within the tagmemic model, a complete phonological analysis includes at least the following:

(a) the segmental phonemes (consonants and vowels) including the aberrant systems of any bilinguals;

(b) the suprasegmental phonemes (tone, stress, length, and perhaps nasalization, laryngealization, etc.);

(c) the syllable, including the distribution of phoneme classes within syllable positions (Pike 1967: 325-41), and also including a constituent analysis of any complex units (K.L. Pike–E.V. Pike, 1947);

(d) the foot or couplet (levels which occur in some languages between syllable and stress group);

(e) the stress group;

(f) the higher levels of the phonological hierarchy such as rhythm group, intonation contour, etc.

A complete analysis of the grammar includes at least the following:

(a) word structure including stem types and stem formation, compounding, and inflection:

(b) phrase structure;

(c) clause structure;

(d) sentence structure; and

(e) discourse structure including a study of contrastive discourse types or genres, with a detailed study of the internal structure of each type.

At each level the functors and their functions are of special interest to the primer maker.

The study of the lexicon includes at least the following: words and word meanings, figures of speech, plot structure in various discourse genres, the vocabulary suitable to various universes of discourse, and specific vocabularies in a wide variety of geographical, social and occupational dialects.

If the language has a traditional written style the analysis should include a comparison of the written style with oral language. There should also be an investigation of the extent to which the written style is familiar to the non-literates. If the written style is relatively unfamiliar, there should be a determination of which styles and genres come closest to the oral style that the illiterate is at home with. In previously unwritten languages, a written style develops very fast as soon as the speakers of the language begin to write it. As such a style develops it should be analyzed in the same way that a traditional written style is analyzed. It is exceedingly important that information concerning written and oral style be available to the primer maker as he chooses the genre and the style for the primer.

In addition to these detailed studies of the language as such, the method requires further information regarding the relationship of all levels of the phonology, grammar, and lexicon to the orthography and spelling. It should be noted that the orthography is far more complex than a simple list of grapheme-phoneme correspondences. At the phonemic level the study includes any phonemes in the language that are not represented in the orthography (some suprasegmental phonemes are frequently omitted from orthographies), any instances of underdifferentiation (where a single symbol is used to represent more than one phoneme), instances of overdifferentiation (in which the same phoneme is written in more than one way). In both underdifferentiation and overdifferentiation it is important to know whether the orthographic choices are completely regular, or whether they are arbitrary, depending on rules which are irrelevant to the language itself.

Ideally the method also draws from extensive psycholinguistic testing. In practice this is done on a very informal basis as part of the basic linguistic analysis, since few field linguists have the competence in psychology to handle laboratory work. Even those who are experienced in such research find it nearly impossible to run any kind of controlled experiment or laboratory type exercise with the freely moving nomadic peoples of the jungles, or the hardworking subsistence farmers of more settled cultures. It is possible, however, to learn a great deal by using case-history techniques, and insightful observation; for examples see Gudschinsky (1958), and Gudschinsky–H. Popovitch–F. Popovitch (1970). The very process of teaching literacy – if done with sensitivity and insight – itself provides an informal laboratory for psycholinguistic observation.

How does the primer maker use this extensive linguistic analysis at each point in his primer making?

Before a primer can be started, there are decisions that must be made:

(1) There must be a list of things which are to be taught in the primer. The first list consists of the phoneme-grapheme correspondences in each position in the minimum pronounceable unit. To make such a list, the primer maker draws from the study of the relationship between the orthography and the phonology of the language. In cases of underdifferentiation his list must include the same symbol repeated in as many different lessons as there are uses of that symbol. In the case of overdifferentiation he must have additional lessons for each way that a given phoneme is represented. In the case of phonemes which are omitted from the orthography, he must plan for lessons in resolving the resultant ambiguities. In the case of phonemes which can occur in several positions within a syllable he must plan lessons for teaching each of those positions (e.g. English *s* in *sit, step, pets*, and *fussy*.)

(2) A second list consists of conventions which are not specifically phoneme-grapheme correspondences. These include word division (which draws upon the grammatical aspect of the orthography study), punctuation (which may relate to phonology, grammar, or lexicon); paragraph markers, titles, capital letters, etc.

(3) A third list includes any arbitrary lexical spellings. These may be the

result of loan words, or the special spelling designed to distinguish homophones. (In English such lexical distinctions form a very large part of the spelling difficulties.)

(4) The fourth is a list of functors. This list will not include all of the functors in the language. Some (like the English *inasmuch*, for example) are too rare and specialized to find a place in the beginning reading materials. Input from the grammar analysis identifies the functors which are obligatory in different discourse types; narrative, for example, may require frequent use of *then, after that*, etc., whereas dialogue may require constant repetition of the first and second person pronouns. The list should also distinguish between functors that belong to contrastive sets (as pronouns, prepositions) and those which are automatic in certain positions (as the third person *-s* on English verbs).

When the primer maker has listed all of the various elements which are to be taught, his next problem is one of sequencing. In which order shall these things be taught? The sequencing is primarily a matter of productive order. It has not proved useful to try to begin with "simple" things and progress to more "difficult" ones (both because we do not know what is easier to learn and because any natural text requires a mixture of kinds of elements). It is, however, exceedingly important that every lesson of the primer have meaningful reading material, and so the highest priority in sequencing is to find productive order which will permit meaningful connected material that is both linguistically adequate and culturally relevant. This means that before the primer maker can organize his lists into a teaching sequence, he must decide which literary genres are most useful for the primer; he must choose between oral and written styles; and he must choose the topics which are of interest to his prospective audience. Within those topics he must choose the vocabulary which will already be known to them. (It should be noted that the primer is not the place to teach *new* vocabulary to the reader. The problem of learning how to read is enough without being required at the same time to learn to understand something that is new to him.) At this point the primer maker is making use of the whole range of lexical studies including studies of dialect and word usage, etc.

In the actual construction of the primer lessons, linguistic information is essential at each point as each primer is tailored specifically to match a specific language.

The choice of keywords depends upon information from the grammatical analysis with regard to the isolatability of words. In some languages single words can be used to label pictures; in others a full sentence is required. In such languages complex morphophonemic changes may limit the possibilities for keywords.

Further information from the phonology and the grammar is required in order to choose the part of the word that can be focused on. In most languages the phonological and grammatical nucleus of the word is suitable as a matrix for the teaching of letter recognition in that it can be pronounced in isolation, and naive speakers are able to focus on it. In other languages where the two criteria do not match, it is necessary to do psycholinguistic testing to find out which part of the word is psychologically most prominent for the naive native speaker.

The problem of the isolatability of part of the word as a pronounceable matrix for letter recognition also depends heavily on the phonological analysis of the language. In many languages a single syllable can be pronounced in isolation. There are other languages in which a single syllable is never pronounced. In the Mixtec languages of Mexico, for example, a syllable is immediately lengthened to a phonemic dissyllabic couplet when it is spoken in isolation. Any attempt to teach by syllables results in confusion deriving from the naive pupil's inability to equate the couplet with which he names the syllable in isolation with the actual single syllables in connected speech. (For a discussion of the use of couplets in this method, see Gudschinsky 1973: 45-48.) Even in languages where the syllable is usually a pronounceable unit, there may be some phonemes which occur only medially in a disyllabic couplet, and must therefore be taught with the couplet as the teaching matrix.

Even after the basic teaching matrix has been chosen, there are still serious linguistic problems in the development of the lesson. The most efficient way of proceeding with the breakdown of the keyword, in languages which permit it, is to isolate the vowel from the teaching unit. There are some languages, however, in which a vowel never appears initially in a word and in fact cannot be pronounced in isolation. There are other languages in which an initial consonant may be removed from a consonant-vowel-consonant syllable leaving a vowel-consonant, but in which the final consonant cannot be removed from the vowel. (A naive speaker of English, for example, can say *it* and *bit* but finds it very difficult to say *bi*.) This is only representative of the whole range of problems which depend upon a linguistic analysis of the constituents of syllables and couplets. These problems include: (a) the difference between clusters of phonemes and unit phonemes; (b) the relationship of nasalization to the vowels with which it occurs (Is it a separate suprasegmental phoneme in its own right? Or simply one feature of the vowel phoneme?); and (c) the psycholinguistic relationship of consonants in clusters; are they of equal weight, or is one dominant and the other a modification? These points are only representative of a wide range of psycholinguistic problems whose solution is vital to the effectiveness of the teaching.

When the primer maker plans the "contrast" step in his decoding section, he is faced with another kind of cultural and linguistic problem. Different cultures apparently see different sets of letters as similar enough to be confused. k, x, and y are not usually on the lists of letters which cause difficulties for new readers. There are cultures, however, in which the "forkedness" of these letters is their predominant characteristic and they are easily confused. Further, in looking for the most relevant contrasts the primer maker must take into account letters which are confused because of phonetic similarity. This also appears to be a psycholinguistic datum.

In word building, the problems of isolatability of words, the meaningfulness of words in isolation, and the internal construction of words are again in focus. The method requires that the words be built from their nuclei with expansion by the addition of margins. This is possible only by building on the linguistic analysis of words.

For the chunking and functor section of the primer lessons, the primer maker needs to know which morphemes of the language are contentives and which are functors. This in itself is no easy question since the functors occupy a continuum from most grammatical and least lexical at one extreme, to almost lexical and minimally grammatical at the other. Some items which are technically functors may in fact be easier to teach as contentives using the decoding skills developed in the first section of the lesson. But even when the primer maker is sure that a particular item should be treated as a functor and taught in this second section of the primer lesson, there are several linguistic parameters to the teaching problem. The steps in the functor lesson must be tailored to take account of whether a given functor is obligatory or optional; whether it is automatic in the position where it is to be used, or contrastive; whether it is unambiguous, or whether it can be mistaken for some other functor or some other contentive in that position.

The steps in this section require that the new functors be introduced in the minimum context which triggers its use. For this, the primer maker leans heavily on the grammatical analysis of the language. Note, for example, that the minimal "triggering" context for a preposition in English is a clause in which the verb requires a locational or directional: "John went *to* school" or "Mary sat *in* the swing". On the other hand, *if* requires a sentence of two clauses: "John will go *if* you like", and *the* requires two sentences as a minimum: "John has a ball. *The* ball is red"

After the minimum triggering environments for the functors have been determined, it is still necessary to determine the minimum meaningful context in which the functor can occur. In the above examples, for example, the following can be isolated and are meaningful in the immediate context of the material from which they are drawn: *to school, in the swing, if you like*, and *the ball*. Such minimum triggering environments and minimum meaningful environments differ very widely from one language to another. It is only input from an adequate grammatical analysis which makes it possible to develop meaningful and effective functor drills.

The story or connected material in each lesson also depends upon input from the linguistic analysis. In the first place the primer maker must choose the style and genre of the primer on the basis of a sociolinguistic study which indicates which styles are used by, and are passively familiar to, the proposed audience.

Further linguistic input concerning the discourse structure is essential for guaranteeing the naturalness of stories, especially under the severe restrictions imposed by the gradual sequential introduction of new letters and functors.

Information from the phonological analysis with regard to the normal rhythm breaks in oral reading, and their relationship to the meaningful units of the grammar, is important in planning the format of the story including the placement of line breaks, and the choice of punctuation.

When the primer maker plans the penmanship, spelling, and creative writing section of the primer lesson, orthography again becomes important to him; he must be aware of the orthography not only from the point of view of the reader, but also from the point of view of the writer. It should be noted that an orthography which underdifferentiates (leaving some phonemic distinctions unmarked) is difficult for the reader because of the potential ambiguity, but is relatively easier for the writer because he has fewer distinctions to keep in mind. On the other hand, an orthography which overdifferentiates (that is, arbitrarily spells the same phoneme in more than one way, or symbolizes allophones) is relatively easier for the reader — who only has to learn to respond to one more symbol in a familiar way — but more difficult for the writer who must remember arbitrary rules in order to spell correctly. It is also the case that spelling homophones differently to indicate the lexical contrast (as in the English *pear, pare, pair*) is a help to the reader who is looking for meaning, but is difficult for the writer who must remember arbitrary rules of spelling.

Each of these complexities in the writer's view of the orthography require additional attention to spelling instruction and practice.

The combinability of various letters will also determine the order in which the pupil is taught to write them, since the purpose is to arrive at freedom in writing and creativity as quickly as possible.

This overview of the contribution of linguistics to my method is suggestive, not exhaustive. As the method is used more and more widely in an increasing variety of languages, the awareness of the role of linguistics grows since each new language presents some fresh problem to be solved.

It is basic to the theoretical foundation of the method that the more nearly the choice and manipulation of the units used in teaching reading approach the naive native speaker's intuitive use of his own language, the more likely it is that in studying the reading lessons he will be able to internalize just those features which are indeed the crucial set for immediate recognition of meaning. (See F. Smith 1971: 3-9, 185-211.)

4

BIBLIOGRAPHY

Abercrombie, David
1963 "Conversation and spoken prose", *English language teaching* 18: 10-6.
Alisjahbana, S. Takdir
1971 "Language policy, language engineering and literacy: Indonesia and Malaysia", in Sebeok (1971: 1087-109).
Allen, Paul David
1972 "What teachers of reading should know about the writing system", in Hodges - Rudolf (1972: 87-99).
Allen, Robert L.
1964 "Better reading through recognition of grammatical relations", *The reading teacher* 18: 194-98
Andersson, Theodore - Mildred Boyer
1970 *Bilingual schooling in the United States*, 2 vol. (Washington, D.C.: Office of Education).
Artley, A. Sterl
1955 "Controversial issues relating to word perception", *The reading teacher* 8: 196-99
Athey, Irene J.
1971a "Language models and reading", *Reading research quarterly* 7: 16-110.
1971b "Synthesis of papers on language development and reading", *Reading research quarterly* 7: 9-15.
Baratz, Joan C.
1969 "Teaching reading in an urban Negro school system", in Baratz - Shuy (1969: 92-116).
1973 "Relationship of Black English to reading: a review of research", in Laffey - Shuy (1973: 101-13).
Baratz, Joan C. - Roger W. Shuy (eds.)
1969 *Teaching Black children to read* (= *Urban language series* 4) (Washington, D.C.: Center for Applied Linguistics).
Bateman, Barbara - Janis Wetherell
1964 "A critique of Bloomfield's linguistic approach to the teaching of reading", *The reading teacher* 18: 98-104.
Bauer, Evelyn
1971 "A history of bilingual education in BIA schools", *Bilingual education for American Indians* 3: 29-32.
Beekman, John
1950 "The use of pre-primer syllable charts in Chol literacy work", *Language learning* 3: 41-50.
Benzies, D.
1940 *Learning our language* (London: Longmans, Green and Co., Ltd.).

Bergman, Richard
1971   "Vowel sandhi and word division in Igede", *Journal of West African languages*
        8: 13-25.
Berry, J.
1952   "Problems in the use of African languages and dialects in education", in:
        African languages and English in education, a report of a meeting of experts
        on the use in education of African languages in relation to English, where
        English is the accepted second language, held at Jos, Nigeria, November (Paris:
        UNESCO Education Clearinghouse), pp; 41-48.
Best, Efraín Morote
1961   "Trabajo y escuela en la selva Peruana", in Elson - Comas (1961: 301-12).
Betts, Emmett Albert
1963   "Reading linguistics", *Education* 83: 515-26.
1964   "Reading: linguistic and psychological bases", in: *Improvement of reading
        through classroom practice* (Ed.: Allen J. Figurel) (=*International Reading
        Association Conference Proceedings* 9) (Newark, Delaware: International
        Reading Association), pp. 20-23.
Biemiller, Andrew
1970   "The development of the use of graphic and contextual information as
        children learn to read", *Reading research quarterly* 6: 75-96.
Bloomfield, Leonard
1942   "Linguistics and reading", *The elementary English review* 19.4: 125-30; 19.5:
        183-86 .
Bloomfield, Leonard - Clarence L. Barnhart
1961   *Let's read: a linguistic approach* (Detroit: Wayne State University Press).
1963   *Let's read*, experimental edition (Bronxville, NY: Clarence L. Barnhart Inc.).
Bolinger, Dwight L.
1946   "Visual morphemes", *Language* 22: 333-40.
Borja, José Jiménez
1958   "Literacy, language and culture", *Fundamental and adult education* 10:
        169-71.
Bormuth, John R.
1968   "New measures of grammatical complexity", in Goodman (1968b: 237-54).
1969   "An operational definition of comprehension instruction", in Goodman -
        Fleming (1969: 48-60).
Bougere, Marguerite Bondy
1969   "Selected factors in oral language related to first-grade reading achievement",
        Reading ressearch quarterly 5: 31-58.
Braun, Carl (ed.)
1971   *Language, reading, and the communication process* (Newark, Delaware:
        International Reading Association).
Brown, D.L.
1971   "Some linguistic dimensions in auditory blending", in Greene (1971: 227-36).
Brown, Eric
1970   "The bases of reading acquisition", *Reading research quarterly* 6: 49-74.
Brown, Roger
1958   *Words and things* (Glencoe, Illinois: The Free Press).
1970   *Psycholinguistics; selected papers*, with Albert Gilmans, Eric Lenneberg,
        Abraham Black *et alii* (New York: The Free Press). [collection of 14 papers,
        published 1954-1970].
1973   *A first language: the early stages* (Cambridge: Harvard University Press).
Brown, Roger - U. Bellugi
1964   "Three processes in the child's acquisition of syntax", *Harvard educational
        review* 34: 133-51.

61

Broz, James, Jr. - Alfred S. Hayes (eds.)
1966   *Linguistics and reading: a selective annotated bibliography for teachers of reading* (Washington, D.C.: Center for Applied Linguistics).
Burke, Carolyn
1973   "Dialect and the reading process", in Laffey - Shuy (1973: 91-100).
Burns, Donald H.
1953   "Social and political implications in the choice of an orthography", *Fundamental and adult education* 5: 80-4.
1971   *Five years of bilingual education in the Andes of Peru* [paper presented at the Andean Language Seminar, Linguistic Institute 1971, State University of New York at Buffalo] [mimeographed]
Butt, Helen
1967   *Integrated literacy method* (Kurukshetra: Kurukshetra University Press).
Calfee, Robert C. - Richard L. Venezky
1969   "Component skills in beginning reading", in Goodman - Fleming (1969: 91-110).
Carroll, John B.
1953   *The study of language: a survey of linguistics and related disciplines in America* (Cambridge: Harvard University Press).
1964   "The analysis of reading instruction: perspectives from psychology and linguistics", in: *Theories of learning and instruction* (Ed.: Ernest R. Hilgard) (= *Sixty-third yearbook of the National Society for the Study of Education*) (Chicago: University of Chicago Press), pp. 336-47.
1970   "The nature of the reading process", in Gunderson (1970: 26-36).
1973   "Language and cognition: current perspectives from linguistics and psychology", in Laffey - Shuy (1973: 173-85).
Carterette, Edward C. - Margaret H. Jones
1965   *Contextual constraints in the language of the child* (Los Angeles: University of California Press).
1968   "Phoneme and letter patterns in children's language", in Goodman (1968b: 103-66).
Chall, Jeanne S.
1967   *Learning to read: the great debate* (New York: McGraw-Hill Book Company).
Chall, Jeanne - Edgar Dale
1948   "A formula for predicting readability", *Educational bulletin* 27: 11-20.
Chapman, Robin - Robert Calfee - Richard Venezky
1970   "Basic language and cognitive skills in kindergartners", in Durr (1970: 17-27).
Chomsky, Carol
1970   "Reading, writing, and phonology", *Harvard educational review* 40: 287-309. [reprinted in F. Smith (1973: 91-104)]
Chomsky, Noam
. 1957   *Syntactic structures* (= *Janua linguarum, series minor* 4) (The Hague: Mouton).
1970   "Phonology and reading", in Levin - Williams (1970: 3-18).
Chomsky, Noam - Morris Halle
1968   *The sound pattern of English* (= *Studies in language*) (New York: Harper and Row).
Conrad, R.
1972   "Speech and reading", in Kavanagh - Mattingly (1972: 205-40).
Coombs, L. Madison
1971   "A summary of pertinent research in bilingual education", *Bilingual education for American Indians* 3: 9-27.
Crowder, Robert G.
1972   "Visual and auditory memory", in Kavanagh - Mattingly (1972: 251-76).
Dale, Edgar
1957   *Bibliography of vocabulary studies*, revised edition by Donald Reichert.

(Columbus, Ohio: Bureau of Educational Research, The Ohio State University). [first edition mimeographed: (1939)]

Dames, J.J.
1965 "What medium of instruction should we use for illiteracy? ", in: *Literacy and progress; handbook for literacy workers* (Nairobi, Kenya: The Literacy Center of Kenya), pp. 124-30.

Danielsson, Bror
1955 *John Hart's works on English orthography and pronunciation* 1: *Biographical and bibliographical introduction, text, and index verborum* (= *Acta Universitatis Stockholmiensis; Stockholm studies in English* 5) (Stockholm: Almqvist and Wiksell). [reproduces Hart (1551)] [2: *Phonology* (= *Acta Universitatis Stockholmiensis; Stockholm studies in English* 11) (1963)]

Davis, Frederick B.
1967 *Philippine language-teaching experiments* (= *Philippine Center for Language Study, monograph series* 5) (Quezon City, Philippines: Alemar Phoenix Publishers).

Dawson, Mildred A.
1969 "How effective is i.t.a. in reading instruction? " in N.B. Smith (1969: 224-37).

Dawson, Mildred A. (ed.)
1971 *Teaching word recognition skills* (Newark, Delaware: International Reading Association).

Dechant, Emerald
1969 *Linguistics, phonics, and the teaching of reading* (Springfield, Ill.: Charles C. Thomas).

Downing, John
1969 "How effective is i.t.a. in reading instruction? pro-challenger", in N.B. Smith (1969: 238-44).
1972 "The orthography factor in literacy acquisition in different languages", *Literacy discussion* 3: 409-27.
1973 *Comparative reading* (New York: The Macmillan Company).

Durr, William K. (ed.)
1970 *Reading difficulties: diagnosis, correction, and remediation* (Newark, Delaware: International Reading Association).

Elliot, A.V.P. - P. Gurrey
1940 *Language teaching in African schools* (London: Longmans).

Elson, Benjamin F. - Juan Comas (eds.)
1961 *A William Cameron Townsend en el vigesimo aniversario del Instituto Lingüístico de Verano* (México, D.F.: Instituto Lingüístico de Verano).

Entwisle, Doris R.
1971 "Implications of language socialization for reading models and for learning to read", *Reading research quarterly* 7: 111-67.

Fairchild, Mildred L. - Kenneth D. Wann
1956 "The educational consultant in another culture", *Teacher's College record* 57: 438-48).

Fasold, Ralph W.
1969 "Orthography in reading materials for Black English speaking children", in Baratz - Shuy (1969: 68-91).

Fearn, Leif - Amelia Martucci
1969 *Reading and the denied learner: an annotated bibliography* (Newark, Delaware: International Reading Association).

Feitelson, Dina
1965 "Structuring the teaching of reading according to major features of the language and its script", *Elementary English* 42: 870-7.

Fernald, Grace M.
1943 *Remedial techniques in basic school subjects* (New York: McGraw-Hill Book

Company, Inc.).
Figurel, J. Allen (ed.)
  1961 *Changing concepts of reading instruction* (= *Proceedings of the International Reading Association Conference* 6) (New York: Scholastic Magazines).
Flesch, Rudolf Franz
  1955 *Why Johnny can't read – and what you can do about it* (New York: Harper and Brothers, Publishers).
Fortune, G.
  1963 "Some possible contributions of linguistics to vernacular language teaching in African schools", in: *Language in Africa* (Ed.: John Spencer) (London: The Syndics of Cambridge University Press), pp. 73-77.
Foster, Philip J.
  1971 "Problems of literacy in Sub-Saharan Africa", in: *Current trends in linguistics* (Ed.: Thomas A. Sebeok) 7: *Linguistics in sub-Saharan Africa* (The Hague: Mouton), pp. 587-617.
Fox, David G.
  1961 "Some psycholinguistic considerations in Quiche literacy", in Elson - Comas (1961: 265-72).
Fries, Charles C.
  1940 *American English grammar; the grammatical structure of present-day American English with special reference to social differences or class dialects* (=*National Council of Teachers of English, English monograph 10*) (New York - London: D. Appleton-Century Company).
  1952 *The structure of English; an introduction to the construction of English sentences* (New York: Harcourt, Brace and Company).
  1962 *Linguistics and reading* (New York: Holt, Rinehart and Winston, Inc. [1963]).
Garvin, Paul L.
  1954 "Literacy as a problem in language and culture", in: *Report of the Fifth Annual Round Table Meeting on linguistics and language studies* (Ed.: Hugo J. Mueller) (= *Georgetown monograph series* 7-8) (Washington D.C.: Georgetown University Press), pp. 117-40.
Gibson, Eleanor J.
  1965 "Learning to read", *Science* 148: 1066-72.
  1970 "The ontogeny of reading", *American psychologist* 25: 136-43.
Gibson, Eleanor J. - Anne Pick - Harry Osser - Marcia Hammond
  1962 "The role of grapheme-phoneme correspondence in the perception of words", *American journal of psychology* 75: 554-70.
Gillooly, William B.
  1969 "How effective is i.t.a. in reading instruction? Con-challenger", in N.B. Smith (1969: 245-53).
Gleason, Henry A., Jr.
  1965 *Linguistics and English grammar* (New York: Holt, Rinehart and Winston, Inc.).
Gleitman, Lila R. - Paul Rozin
  1973 "Teaching reading by use of a syllabary", *Reading research quarterly* 8: 447-83.
Goodman, Kenneth S.
  1965 "Dialect barriers to reading comprehension", *Elementary English* 42: 853-60. [reprinted in Baratz - Shuy (1969: 14-28)]
  1967 "Reading: a psycholinguistic guessing game", *Journal of the reading specialists* 6.4: 126-35. [reprinted in Singer - Ruddell (1970: 259-72)]
  1968a "The psycholinguistic nature of the reading process", in Goodman (1968b: 13-26).
  1969a "Analysis of oral reading miscues: applied psycholinguistics", *Reading*

research quarterly 5: 9-30. ⌊reprinted in F. Smith (1973: 158-76)⌋
1969b "Is the linguistic approach an improvement in reading? Pro-challenger", in N.B. Smith (1969: 268-76).
1969c "Words and morphemes in reading", in Goodman - Fleming (1969: 25-33).
1970a "Dialect rejection and reading: a response", *Reading research quarterly* 5: 600-3.
1970b "Psycholinguistic universals in the reading process", *Journal of typographic research* 4: 103-10. [reprinted in F. Smith (1973: 21-27)]
1971 "On the psycholinguistic method of teaching reading", *Elementary school journal* 1971: 177-81. [reprinted in F. Smith (1973: 177-82)]
1972 "The reading process: theory and practice", in Hodges - Rudorf (1972: 143-59).
1973 "The 13th way to make learning to read difficult: a reaction to Gleitman and Rozin", *Reading research quarterly* 8: 484-93.
Goodman, Kenneth S. (ed.)
1968b *The psycholinguistic nature of the reading process* (Detroit: Wayne State University Press). [= papers presented at a symposium held at Wayne State, May 3-5, 1965]
Goodman, Kenneth S. - James T. Fleming (eds.)
1969 *Psycholinguistics and the teaching of reading* (Newark, Delaware: International Reading Association).
Goodman, Yetta M.
1972 "Qualitative reading miscue analysis for teacher training", in Hodges - Rudorf (1972: 160-65).
Goodman, Yetta M. - Kenneth S. Goodman
1967 *Linguistics and the teaching of reading; an annotated bibliography* (Newark, Delaware: International Reading Association).
1971 *Linguistics, psycholinguistics and the teaching of reading; an annotated bibliography* (Newark, Delaware: International Reading Association).
Gough, Philips B.
1972 "One second of reading", in Kavanagh - Mattingly (1972: 331-58).
Gray, William S.
1956 *The teaching of reading and writing* (= *Monographs on fundamental education* 10) (Paris: UNESCO).
Greene, Frank P. (ed.)
1971 *Reading: the right to participate* (= *Twentieth yearbook of the National Reading Conference*) (Milwaukee, Wisconsin: The National Reading Conference, Inc.).
Gudschinsky, Sarah C.
1951 *Handbook of literacy* (Santa Ana, California: Summer Institute of Linguistics). [revised editions: (Norman, Okl.: Summer Institute of Linguistics, University of Oklahoma 1953, 1957)]
1952 "Solving the Mazateco reading problem", *Language learning* 4: 61-65.
1958 "Native reactions to tones and words in Mazatec", *Word* 14: 338-45.
1959a "Recent trends in primer construction", *Fundamental and adult education* 11: 367-96.
1959b "Toneme representation in Mazatec orthography", *Word* 15: 446-52.
1968 "The relationship of language and linguistics to reading", *Kivung* 1: 146-52.
1970a "More on formulating efficient orthographies", *The Bible translator* 21: 21-25. [review of Powlisson (1968)]
1970b "Psycholinguistics and reading: diagnostic observation", in Durr (1970: 154-63).
1972 "The nature of the writing system: pedagogical implications", in Hodges - Rudorf (1972: 100-12).

1973   *A manual of literacy for preliterate peoples* (Papua New Guinea: Summer
        Institute of Linguistics).
1974   "Linguistics and literacy". [to appear in: *Current trends in linguistics* (Ed.:
        Thomas A. Sebeok) 12: *Linguistics and adjacent sciences* (The Hague:
        Mouton)]
Gudschinsky, Sarah C. - Harold Popovitch - Frances Popovitch
1970   "Native reaction and phonetic similarity in Maxakali phonology", *Language*
        46: 77-88.
Gunderson, Doris V. (ed.)
1970   *Language and reading: an interdisciplinary approach* (Washington, D.C.: Center
        for Applied Linguistics).
Gwyther-Jones, Roy E.
1971   "Some literacy problems in the Territory of Papua and New Guinea", *Literacy
        discussion* 2: 7-16.
Hall, MaryAnne
1972   *The language experience approach for the culturally disadvantaged* (Newark,
        Delaware: International Reading Association).
Halle, Morris
1969   "Some thoughts on spelling", in Goodman - Fleming (1969: 17-24).
Halvorson, Marian
1967   "Primer writing for adult literacy in Bantu languages", *Linguistic reporter:
        newsletter for the Center for Applied Linguistics* 9: 1-2.
Hansen, Duncan – Theodore Rodgers
1968   "An exploration of psycholinguistic units in initial reading", in Goodman
        (1968b: 59-102).
Harris, Joy Kinslow
1968   "Linguistics and Aboriginal education", *Australian Territories* 8: 24-34.
Hart, John
1551   *The opening of the unreasonable writing of our inglish toung.* [reproduced in
        Danielsson (1955)]
Hayes, Alfred S.
1964   *Linguistic priorities in developing literacy teaching material in the mother
        tongue or local lingua franca.* [paper presented at the UNESCO meeting of
        experts on the use of the mother tongue for literacy, Ibadan]
Hayes, Alfred S. (ed.)
1965   *Recommendations of the Work Conference on Literacy*, held for the Agency
        for International Development, United States Department of State, at Airlie
        House, Warrenton, Virginia, May 23-28, 1964 (Washington, D.C.: Center for
        Applied Linguistics).
Heath, Shirley Brice
1972   *Telling tongues* (New York: Teachers College Press).
Henderson, Edmund H.
1972   "Linguistics, thought, and reading", in Hodges - Rudorf (1972: 216-23).
Hildreth, Gertrude
1964   "Linguistic factors in early reading instruction", *The reading teacher* 18:
        172-78.
Hodges, Richard E. - E. Hugh Rudorf (eds.)
1972   *Language and learning to read: what teachers should know about language*
        (Boston: Houghton Mifflin Company).
Holden, Majorie H. - Walter H. MacGinitie
1972   "Children's conceptions of word boundaries in speech and print", *Journal of
        educational psychology* 63: 551-57.
Huey, Edmund Burke
1908   *The psychology and pedagogy of reading* (New York: The Macmillan Co.).

[reprinted: (Cambridge, Mass.: M.I.T. Press 1968)] [cf. Kolers (1968)]
Hughes, Ann
1969 "Is the linguistic approach an improvement in reading instruction? Con-challenger", in N.B. Smith (1969: 227-82).
Hunt, Chester L.
1966 "Language choice in a multilingual society", *Sociological inquiry* 36: 240-53.
Ives, Sumner - Josephine P. Ives
1970 "Linguistics and reading", in Marckwardt (1970: 243-63).
John, Vera P. - Vivian M. Horner - Tomi D. Berney
1970 "Story retelling: a study of sequential speech in young children", in Levin - Williams (1970: 246-62).
Jones, Margaret Hubbard
1968 "Some thoughts on perceptual units in language processing", in Goodman (1968b: 41-58).
Kavanagh, James F. - Ignatius G. Mattingly (eds.)
1972 *Language by ear and by eye: the relationships between speech and reading* (Cambridge, Massachusetts: The Massachusetts Institute of Technology Press).
Kehoe, Monika
1963 "The language dilemma in Ethiopia", *Oversea education* 24: 162-65.
Kliger, Samuel
1971 "Transformational-generative grammar and literacy education", *Literacy discussion* 3: 135-49.
Klima, Edward S.
1972 "How alphabets might reflect language", in Kavanagh - Mattingly (1972: 57-80).
Kolers, Paul A.
1968a "Reading temporally and spatially transformed text", in Goodman (1968b: 27-40).
1968b "Introduction", in E.B. Huey, *The psychology and pedagogy of reading*, second edition (Cambridge, Mass.: M.I.T. Press 1968), pp. xiii-xxxix. [cf. Huey (1908)]
1969 "Reading is only incidentally visual", in Goodman - Fleming (1969: 8-16).
1970 "Three stages of reading", in Levin - Williams (1970: 90-118). [reprinted in F. Smith (1973: 28-49)]
Labov, William
1967 "Some sources of reading problems for Negro speakers of Nonstandard English", in: *New directions in elementary English*, papers collected from the 1966 spring institutes on the elementary language arts of the National Council of Teachers of English (Ed.: A. Frazier) (Champaihn, Illinois: National Council of Teachers of English), pp. 140-67. [reprinted in Baratz - Shuy (1969: 29-67)]
1970 "The reading of the -*ed* suffix", in Levin - Williams (1970: 222-45).
Labov, William *et alii*
1969 *A study of the Non-standard English of Negro and Puerto Rican speakers in New York City* (= *Final report, U.S. Office of Education Cooperative Research Project No. 3288*), 2 vol. (Washington, D.C.: Center for Applied Linguistics).
Laffey, James L. - Roger Shuy (eds.)
1973 *Language differences: do they interfere?* (Newark, Delaware: International Reading Association).
Larudee, Faze
1972 "Creative reading for world literacy", *Literacy discussion* 3: 428-51.
Lastra, Yolanda
1968 "Literacy", in: *Current trends in linguistics* (Ed.: Thomas A. Sebeok) 4:

Ibero-American and Caribbean linguistics (The Hague: Mouton), pp. 415-63.
Laubach, Frank C.
1937 "The Philippines' literacy method", *Books for Africa* 7: 35-41.
1947 *Teaching the world to read; a handbook for literacy campaigns* (New York: Friendship Press).
Lavondes, Henri
1971 "Language policy, language engineering and literacy: French Polynesia", in Sebeok (1971: 1 110-28).
Leaverton, Lloyd
1973 "Dialectal readers: rationale, use, and value", in Laffey - Shuy (1973: 114-26).
Lefevre, Carl A.
1961 "Reading instruction related to primary language learning: a linguistic view", *Journal of developmental reading* 4: 147-58
1964 *Linguistics and the teaching of reading* (= *Curriculum and methods in education*) (New York: McGraw-Hill Book Company). [multilith edition: (1962)]
Leibowitz, Arnold H.
1971 "A history of language instruction in American Indian schools: the imposition of English by government policy", *Bilingual education for American Indians* 3: 1-6.
Lenneberg, Eric H.
1967 *Biological foundations of language*, with appendices by Noam Chomsky and Otto Marx (new York: John Wiley and Sons, Inc.).
Levin, Harry - Eleanor L. Kaplan
1970 "Grammatical structure and reading", in Levin - Williams (1970: 119-33).
Levin, Harry - Nancy S. Meltzer (eds.)
1964-68 *Project literacy reports* 1-9 (Ithaca: Project Literacy, Cornell Univeristy). [mimeographed]
Levin, Harry - Joanna P. Williams (eds.)
1970 *Basic studies on reading* (New York: Basic Books, Inc.).
Lloyd, Donald J.
1963 "Sub-cultural patterns which affect language and reading development", in Weiss (1963: 37-54).
Longacre, Robert E.
1964 *Grammar discovery procedures* (= *Janua linguarum, series minor* 33) (The Hague: Mouton).
McCullough, Constance M.
1965 *Preparation of textbooks in the mother tongue* (New Delhi: National Institute of Education).
1972 "What should the reading teacher know about language and thinking? ", in Hodges - Rudorf (1972: 202-15).
McDavid, Raven I.
1961 "The role of the linguist in the teaching of reading", in Figurel (1961: 253-55).
1964 "Dialectology and the teaching of reading", *The reading teacher* 18: 206-13. [reprinted in Baratz - Shuy (1969: 1-13)]
McGuffey, William Holmes
1836-57 *The eclectic reader*, 6 vol. (Cincinnati: Truman & Smith). [1,2: (1836); 3,4: (1837); 5: (1844); 6: (1857)] [a more recent edition: *McGuffey's new first-sixth eclectic reader*, 6 vol. (New York - Cincinnati: American Books Company 1866-85; reprinted: (1930).
McLeod, John
1967 "Some psycholinguistic correlates of reading disability in young children", *Reading research quarterly* 2: 5-32.

68

McNinch, George
  1971 "Auditory perceptual factors and measured first-grade reading achievement",
         Reading research quarterly 6: 472-92.
Marckwardt, Albert H. (ed.)
  1970 *Linguistics in school programs* (= *Yearbook of the National Society for the*
         Study of Education 69.2) (Chicago: The University of Chicago Press).
Marquardt, William F.
  1964 "Language interference in reading", *The reading teacher* 18: 214-18.
  1965 "Linguistics and reading instruction: contributions and implications", in
         Robinson (1965: 112-21).
Mattingly, Ignatius G.
  1972 "Reading, the linguistic process, and linguistic awareness", in Kavanagh –
         Mattingly (1972: 133-48).
Melmed, Paul Jay
  1973 "Black English phonology: the question of reading interference", in Laffey -
         Shuy (1973: 70-85).
Miller, George A.
  1951 *Language and communication* (New York: McGraw-Hill Book Company, Inc.).
  1965 "Some preliminaries to psycholinguistics", *American psychologist* 20: 15-20.
         [reprinted in F. Smith (1973: 10-20)]
Modiano, Nancy
  1968 "Bilingual education for children of linguistic minorities", *América Indígena*
         28: 405-14.
  1973 "Juanito's reading problems: foreign language interference and reading skill
         acquisition", in Laffey - Shuy (1973: 29-39).
Mountain, Lee
  1971 "Intonation for beginners", in Braun (1971: 149-54).
Neijs, Karel
  1958 *An experimental course in adult literacy* (= *South Pacific Commission*
         technical paper 114) (Noumea, New Caledonia: South Pacific Commission).
  1960 "Some considerations on the making of adult literacy primers", *Fundamental*
         and adult education 12: 41-58.
Nida, Eugene A.
  1947 *Bible translating* (New York: American Bible Society).
  1949 "Approaching reading through the native language", *Language learning* 2:
         16-20.
  1967a "Linguistic dimensions of literacy and literature", in Shacklock (1967:
         142-61).
  1967b "Sociological dimensions of literacy and literature", in Shacklock (1967:
         127-41).
Olsen, Hans G.
  1968 "Linguistics and materials for beginning reading instruction", in Goodman
         (1968b: 271-88).
Orata, Pedro T.
  1953 "The Iloilo experiment in education through the vernacular", in: *The use of*
         vernacular languages in education (= *Monographs on fundamental education* 8)
         (Paris: UNESCO), pp. 123-31.
Osgood, Charles E. - Thomas A. Sebeok (eds.)
  1964 *Psycholinguistics: a survey of theory and research problems* (= *Indiana*
         University studies in the history and theory of linguistics) (Bloomington:
         Indiana University Press).
Pike, Kenneth L.
  1947 *Phonemics: a technique for reducing languages to writing* (ann Arbor:
         University of Michigan Press).
  1967 *Language in relation to a unified theory of the structure of human behavior*,

second revised edition (=*Janua linguarum, series major* 24) (The Hague: Mouton). [preliminary edition in 3 vol.: (Santa Ana, California: The Summer Institute of Linguistics, Inc. 1954-60)]

Pike, Kenneth L. - Eunice V. Pike
1947 "Immediate constituents of Mazateco syllables", *International journal of American linguistics* 13: 78-91.

Pival, Jean - George Faust
1965 "Toward improved reading instruction: a discussion of variation in pronunciation linked with stress", *Elementary English* 42: 861-65.

Posner, Michael I. - Joe L. Lewis - Carol Conrad
1972 "Component processes in reading: a performance analysis", in Kavanagh - Mattingly (1972: 159-92).

Powlison, Paul S.
1968 "Bases for formulating an efficient orthography", *The Bible translator* 19: 74-91. [rec.: Gudschinsky (1970a)]

Pulgram, Ernest
1951 "Phoneme and grapheme: a parallel", *Word* 7: 15-20.

Ramanauskas, Sigita
1972 "The responsiveness of cloze readability measures to linguistic variables operating over segments of text longer than a sentence", *Reading research quarterly* 8: 72-91

Read, Charles
1971 "Pre-School children's knowledge of English phonology", *Harvard educational review* 41: 1-34.

Reed, David W.
1965 "A theory of language, speech, and writing", *Elementary English* 42: 845-51.
1970a "A glance at the linguistic organization of elementary reading textbooks", in Gunderson (1970: 98-106).
1970b "Linguistic forms and the process of reading", in Levin - Williams (1970: 19-29).

Reed, David W. - Jesse O. Sawyer
1970 "Linguistic considerations in reading disability", in Durr (1970: 143-53).

Robinett, Ralph F.
1965 "Constructing a developmental reading program for children who speak other languages: some basic criteria", in: *On teaching English to speakers of other languages* (ed.: Carol J. Kreidler) (Champaign, Illinois: National Council of Teachers of English).

Robinson, H. Alan (ed.)
1963 *Reading and the language arts* (=*Proceedings of the Annual Conference on Reading held at the University of Chicago* 25, = *The school review – The elementary school journal, Supplementary educational monographs* 93) (Chicago: University of Chicago Press).
1965 *Recent developments in reading* (=*Proceedings of the Annual Conference on Reading held at the University of Chicago* 27, = *The school review – The elementary school journal, Supplementary educational monographs* 95) (Chicago: The University of Chicago Press).

Rosen, Carl L. - Philips D. Ortego
1969 *Issues in language and reading instruction of Spanish-speaking children: an annotated bibliography* (Newark, Delaware: International Reading Association).

Rozin, Paul - Susan Poritsky - Raina Sotsky
1971 "American children with reading problems can easily learn to read English represented by Chinese characters", *Science* 171: 1264-67. [reprinted in F. Smith (1973: 105-15)]

Ruddell, Robert B.
   1968   "The relation of regularity of grapheme-phoneme correspondences and of
           language structure to achievement in first-grade reading", in Goodman
           (1968b: 255-70).
   1969   "Psycholinguistic implications for a system of communication model", in
           Goodman - Fleming (1969: 61-78). [reprinted in Singer - Ruddell (1970:
           239-58)]
   1970   "Language acquisition and the reading process", in Singer - Ruddell (1970:
           1-19).
Ruddell, Robert B. - Helen G. Bacon
   1972   "The nature of reading: language and meaning", in Hodges - Rudorf (1971:
           169-88).
Ryan, Ellen Bouchard - Melvyn I. Semmel
   1969   "Reading as a constructive language process", Reading research quarterly 5:
           59-83.
Rystrom, Richard C.
   1969   "Testing Negro-Standard English dialect differences", Reading research
           quarterly 4: 500-11.
   1970a "Dialect training and reading: a further look", Reading research quarterly 5:
           581-99.
   1970b "Negro speech and others: a reply", Reading research quarterly 6: 123-25.
   1973   "Reading, language, and nonstandard dialects: a research report", in Laffey -
           Shuy (1973: 86-90).
Sadler, Wesley
   1959   "The Loma literacy programme", International review of missions 48: 318-24.
Sapir, Edward
   1949   "The psychological reality of phonemes", in: Selected writings of Edward
           Sapir in language, culture, and personality (Ed.: David G. Mandelbaum)
           (Berkeley and Los Angeles: University of California Press), pp. 46-60.
           [published originally in French: "La réalité psychologique des phonèmes",
           Journal de psychologie normale et pathologique 30 (1933): 247-65]
Saporta, Sol (ed.)
   1961   Psycholinguistics: a book of readings, prepared with the assistance of Jarvin R.
           Bastian (New York: Holt, Rinehart and Winston).
Savin, Harris B.
   1972   "What the child knows about speech when he starts to read", in Kavanagh -
           Mattingly (1972: 319-26).
Savin, Harris B. - Thomas G. Bever
   1970   "The nonperceptual reality of the phoneme", Journal of verbal learning and
           verbal behavior 9: 295-302.
Schlesinger, I.M.
   1968   Sentence structure and the reading process (= Janua linguarum, series minor
           69) (The Hague: Mouton).
Scholes, Robert J.
   1970   "On functors and contentives in children's imitations of word strings", Journal
           of verbal learning and verbal behavior 9: 167-70.
Sebeok, Thomas A. (ed.)
   1971   Current trends in linguistics 8: Linguistics in Oceania, 2 vol. (The Hague:
           Mouton).
Sebesta, Sam Leaton
   1968   "My son, the linguist and reader", Elementary English 45: 233-35, 242.
Seligman, Martin E.P. - Joanne L. Hager (eds.)
   1972   Biological boundaries of learning (New York: Appleton-Century-Crofts).

Serwer, Blanche E.
    1969   "Linguistic support for a method of teaching beginning reading to black
            children", *Reading research quarterly* 4: 449-67.
Seymour, Dorothy Z.
    1973   "Neutralizing the effect of the nonstandard dialect", in Laffey - Shuy (1973:
            149-62).
Shacklock, Floyd (ed.)
    1967   *World literacy manual* (New York: Committee on World Literacy and
            Christian Literature).
Shankweiler, Donald - Isabelle Y. Liberman
    1972   "Misreading: a search for causes", in Kavanagh - Mattingly (1972: 293-318).
Shell, Olive
    1971   "Additional notes to 'A bilingual experiment in the jungles of Peru' ",
            Literacy discussion 2: 25-32.
Shuy, Roger W.
    1969a   "A linguistic background for developing beginning reading materials for black
            children", in Baratz - Shuy (1969: 117-37).
    1969b   "Some language and cultural differences in a theory of reading", in Goodman -
            Fleming (1969: 34-47).
    1973   "Nonstandard dialect problems: an overview", in Laffey - Shuy (1973: 3-16).
Sibayan, Bonifacio P.
    1971   "Language policy, language engineering, and literacy: the Philippines", in
            Sebeok (1971: 1038-62).
Singer, Harry
    1971   "Theories, models, and strategies for learning to read", in: *Reading: the right
            to participate* (Ed.: Frank P. Greene) (= *20th yearbook of the National
            Reading Conference, Inc.*) (Milwaukee, Wis.: Reading Center, Marquette
            University), pp. 93-113.
Singer, Harry - Robert B. Ruddell (eds.)
    1970   *Theoretical models and processes of reading*, with a foreword by James F.
            Kavanagh (Newark, Delaware: International Reading Association).
Sjoberg, Andrée F.
    1966   "Sociocultural and linguistic factors in the development of writing systems
            for pre-literate peoples", in: *Sociolinguistics: Proceedings of the U.C.L.A.
            Sociolinguistics Conference*, Los Angeles and Lake Arrowhead, Calif., (Ed.:
            William Bright) (= *Janua linguanum, series major* 20), pp. 260-76.
Smalley, William A. *et alii*
    1964   *Orthography studies; articles on new writing systems* [= *Helps for translators*
            6) (London: United Bible Societies).
Smith, Frank
    1971   *Understanding reading; a psycholinguistic analysis of reading and learning to
            read* (New York: Holt, Rinehart and Winston, Inc.).
    1973a   *Psycholinguistics and reading* (New York: Holt, Rinehart and Winston, Inc.).
    1973b   "Alphabetic writing – a linguistic compromise? ", in F. Smith (1973a:
            116-30).
Smith, Frank - Deborah Lott Holmes
    1971   "The independence of letter, word, and meaning identification in reading",
            Reading research quarterly 6: 394-415. [reprinted in F. Smith (1973a: 50-69)]
Smith, Henry Lee, Jr.
    1956   *Linguistic science and the teaching of English* (Cambridge: Harvard University
            Press). [= The Inglis lecture 1954]
Smith, Nila Banton
    1934   *American reading instruction* (New York: Silver, Burdett and Company).
Smith, Nila Banton (ed.)
    1969   *Current issues in reading* (= *Proceedings of the thirteenth annual convention,*

International Reading Association 13.2) (Newark, Delaware: International Reading Association).

Soderbergh, Ragnhild
1971 *Reading in early childhood: a linguistic study of a Swedish preschool child's gradual acquisition of reading ability* (Stockholm: Almqvist and Wiksell).

Soffietti, James P.
1955 "Why children fail to read: a linguistic analysis", *The Harvard educational review* 25: 63-84

Stauffer, Russell G. (ed.)
1964 *Linguistics and reading* (Newark, Delaware: International Reading Association). [= *The reading teacher* 18: 170-248]

Steinberg, Danny D.
1973 "Phonology, reading, and Chomsky and Halle's optimal orthography", *Journal of psycholinguistic research* 2: 239-58.

Stevens, Warren D.
1963 *A review of the national mass literacy program of the government of Mali with recommendations for communications media facilities: Agency for International Development Consultant's report, June 1963* (Bloomington: Indiana University, Division of Educational Media). [mimeographed]

Stewart, William A.
1969 "On the use of Negro dialect in the teaching of reading", in Baratz - Shuy (1969: 156-219).

Strickland, Ruth G.
1963 *The contribution of structural linguistics to the teaching of reading, writing, and grammar in the elementary school* (= *Bulletin of the School of Education, Indiana University* 40.1) (Bloomington: Indiana University, School of Education [1964]).

Tatham, Susan Masland
1970 "Reading comprehension of materials written with select oral language patterns: a study at grades two and four", *Reading research quarterly* 5: 402-26.

Torrey, Jane W.
1969 "Learning to read without a teacher: a case study", *Elementary English* 46: 550-6. [reprinted in F. Smith (1973: 147-57)]

Townsend, Elaine Mielke
1948 "Accelerating literacy by piecemeal digestion of the alphabet", *Language learning* 1.3: 9-19.
1952 "The construction and use of readers for Aymara Indians", *Fundamental and adult education* 4.4: 21-5.

Trager, George L. - Henry Lee Smith, Jr.
1951 *An outline of English structure* (= *Studies in linguistics, occasional papers* 3) (Norman, Oklahoma: Battenburg Press).

Trifonovitch, Gregory J.
1971 "Language policy, language engineering, and literacy: Trust Territory of the Pacific Islands", in Sebeok (1971: 1063-87).

Tucker, A.N.
1952 "The linguistic aspects of mass literacy movements", in: *Symposium on popular education – Symposium sur l'éducation populaire, Leiden, 1952; French North-Africa – Tropical Africa – Indonesia before the Second World War – Netherlands New Guinea, organized by the Afrika-Instituut, Studiëcentrum Leiden, 31 March - 2 April 1952* (Leiden: Universitaire Pers Leiden, 1953), pp. 74-93.
1971 "Orthographic systems and conventions in Sub-Saharan Africa", in: *Current trends in linguistics* (Ed.: Thomas A Sebeok) 7: *Linguistics in sub-Saharan*

Africa (The Hague: Mouton), pp. 618-53.
UNESCO
    1953   *The use of vernacular languages in education* (= *Monographs on fundamental education* 8) (Paris: UNESCO).
Venezky, Richard L.
    1967   "English orthography: its graphical structure and its relation to sound", *Reading research quarterly* 2: 75-105.
    1970a "Linguistics and spelling", in Marckwardt (1970: 264-74).
    1970b "Regularity in reading and spelling", in Levin - Williams (1970: 30-42).
    1970c *The structure of English orthography* (= *Janua linguarum, series minor* 82) (The Hague: Mouton).
Venezky, Richard L. - Robert C. Calfee
    1970   "The reading competency model", in Singer - Ruddell (1970: 273-91).
Venezky, Richard L. - Robin S. Chapman
    1973   "Is learning to read dialect bound? ", in Laffey - Shuy (1973: 62-9).
Walker, Willard
    1969   "Notes on native writing systems and the design of native literacy programs", *Anthropological linguistics* 11: 148-66.
Wallis, Ethel E.
    1952   "Using linguistic analyses in literacy methods in Mexico", *Fundamental and adult education* 4: 16-21.
    1956   "Sociolinguistics in relation to Mezquital Otomi transition education", in: *Estudios anthropológicos publicados en homenaje al doctor Manuel Gamio* (México, D.F.: Sociedad Mexicana de Anthropologia, Universidad Nacional Autónoma de México), pp. 523-35.
Wardhaugh, Ronald
    1969a "Is the linguistic approach an improvement in reading instruction? ", in Smith (1969: 254-67).
    1969b *Reading: a linguistic perspective* (New York: Harcourt, Brace and World, Inc.).
    1969c "The teaching of phonics and comprehension: a linguistic evaluation", in Goodman - Fleming (1969: 79-90).
    1971a "Linguistics and phonics", in Braun (1971: 105-12).
    1971b "Theories of language acquisition in relation to beginning reading instruction", *Reading research quarterly* 7: 168-94.
Wares, Iris Mills
    1965   *Linguistic and related problems in Mexican Indian literacy* (The University of Texas). [Master's thesis]
Warren, Richard M.
    1971   "Identification times for phonemic components of graded complexity and for spelling of speech", *Perception and psychophysics* 9: 345-49.
Watts, Betty H. (ed.)
    1971   *Report of the National Workshop on Aboriginal Education priorities for action and research* (Brisbane: University of Queensland, Department of Education).
Weaver, Wendell W. - Albert J. Kingston
    1972   "Modeling the effects of oral language upon reading language", *Reading research quarterly* 7: 613-27.
Weber, Rose-Marie
    1970a "A linguistic analysis of first-grade reading errors", *Reading research quarterly* 5: 427-51.
    1970b "First-graders' use of grammatical context in reading", in Levin - Williams (1970: 147-63).
    1973   "Dialect differences in oral reading: an analysis of errors", in Laffey - Shuy (1973: 47-61).

Weir, Ruth H. - Richard Venezky
1968   "Spelling-to-sound patterns", in Goodman (1968b: 185-200).
Weiss, Bernard J. (ed.)
1963   *Language, linguistics and school programs, proceedings of the Spring Institutes, 1963 of the National Council of Teachers of English; Louisville, Ky., March 3-9 – Atlantic City, N.J., April 21-27* (Champaign, Illinois: National Council of Teachers of English).
Whipple, Guy Montrose (ed.)
1925   *Report of the National Committee on Reading* (= *Twenty-fourth yearbook of the National Society for the Study of Education*) (Bloomington: Public School Publishing Co.).
Whiteley, W.H. (ed.)
1971   *Language use and social change: problems of multilingualism with special reference to Eastern Africa; studies presented and discussed at the ninth International African Seminar at University College, Dar es Salaam, December 1968* (London: Oxford University Press).
Wise, Mary Ruth
1971   "A bilingual experiment in the jungle of Peru", *Literacy discussion* 2: 17-24.
Wolff, Hans
1954   *Nigerian orthography* (Zaria, Nigeria: North Regional Adult Education Office).
Wolfram, Walter A.
1970   "Sociolinguistic alternatives in teaching reading to nonstandard speakers", *Reading research quarterly* 6: 9-33.
Wolfram, Walter A. - Ralph W. Fasold
1969   "Toward reading materials for speakers of Black English: three linguistically appropriate passages", in Baratz - Shuy (1969: 138-55).
Wonderly, William L.
1961   "Some factors of meaningfulness in reading matter for inexperienced readers", in Elson - Comas (1961: 387-97).
Wurm, S.A.
1966   "Language and literacy", in: *New Guinea on the threshold* (Ed.: E.K. Fisk) (Canberra: Australian National University), pp. 135-48.
1971   "Language policy, language engineering and literacy: New Guinea and Australia", in Sebeok (1971: 1025-38).
Yngve, V.H.
1960   "A model and an hypothesis for language structure", *Proceedings of the American Philosophical Society* 104: 444-66.
Young, Robert
1953   "To read and write native languages", in: *Education for cultural change* (ed.: W. Beatty) (Washington, D.C.: U.S. Department of Interior, Bureau of Indian Affairs), pp. 408-14.
Zuck, Louis V. - Yetta M. Goodman
1971   *Social class and regional dialects: their relationship to reading: an annotated bibliography* (Newark, Delaware: International Reading Association).

Bilingual education for American Indians – curriculum bulletin of the Bureau of Indian Affairs (correspondence concerning distribution and editorial content of this bulletin should be directed to Mr. Robert Rebert, Language Arts Branch, Division of Educational Planning and Development, Bureau of Indian Affairs, 123 Fourth Street, S.W., Albuquerque, New Mexico, 87103).

Notes on literacy – the literacy house – organ of The Summer Institute of Linguistics, Inc., Huntington Beach, California; started by Sarah Gudschinsky, now edited by Margaret Wendell and published at irregular intervals.

INDEX

Wurm, S. A. 39

Yngve, V. H. 27

Zuni 33